C000018060

LISA APPIGNANESI was bo... grew up in Paris and Montreal be... twenties. Her many prizewinning books, ... fiction, include *Freud's Women* (with John Forrester), *Losing the Dead*, *Mad, Bad and Sad* and *Trials of Passion*. She is known as a cultural commentator, writes for the *New York Review of Books*, has been President of English PEN, chair of the Freud Museum London and of the Man Booker International Prize. She is currently chair of the Royal Society of Literature.

Praise for *Everyday Madness*:

'*Everyday Madness* offers a brilliant theory and definition of a modern malady . . . in identifying a previously undescribed territory, Lisa Appignanesi has wonderfully invented a previously unwritten form'
Adam Thirlwell

'Keen-eyed, unflinching in her honesty, Lisa Appignanesi carries us down into the depths . . . With piercing insight and many moments of intense poignancy, she illuminates the complexity and costs of a remarkable and passionate journey'
Marina Warner

'Wonderful, moving, extraordinary. It is sui generis. I feel enormously privileged to have read it . . . Bravo, bravo'
Edmund de Waal

'Thoughtful, challenging, illuminating, truthful and moving. We all bear losses. Lisa Appignanesi breaks the isolation and helps us endure them'
Susie Orbach

'By deftly moving between the personal and the public, between childhood and adulthood, between the immediacy of feeling and the distance of reflection, Lisa Appignanesi constructs an anatomy of grief and its frequent but discomfiting attendant: rage'
Siri Hustvedt

'You will find all of life in this rewarding, scholarly and entertaining conversation about freedom, Freud, fury, enduring love, and how mythic and modern families haunt each other'
Deborah Levy

'Searingly precise, analytical and honest, *Everyday Madness* is a literary meditation on grief, rage and truth, and the complex interaction between them. This is a courageous and original book'
Sigrid Rausing

'A ragged, stop-start quality, often feeling like a conversation, at times an argument, with the reader, and is all the more engaging for it'
Guardian

'*Everyday Madness* is supple, powerful and remarkably solipsistic; Appignanesi meditates with great wisdom and fierce honesty on "the puzzle that the self perennially is" in a memoir that begins in opaqueness and ends in clarity'
TLS

'A brave and compelling book'   *New Statesman*

'This book is astonishingly compelling . . . It is a running reflection on grief and anger combined, the one provoking the other, in a book needed by so many people . . . her reflection will help many bereaved women plot their journey, as she has charted hers'   *Jewish Chronicle*

'Appignanesi's personal condition chimed with the times. Observing the fury unleashed during the banking crisis, the election of Donald Trump, Brexit and the Me Too movement, she understands more deeply how these rages are driven by fear and loss . . . She's good on the historic suppression and mockery of female rage and the rise of misogyny online'
    Daily Telegraph

By the same author

EVERYDAY MADNESS

On Grief, Anger, Loss and Love

LISA APPIGNANESI

4th ESTATE • *London*

4th Estate
An imprint of HarperCollins*Publishers*
1 London Bridge Street
London SE1 9GF
www.4thEstate.co.uk

First published in Great Britain by 4th Estate in 2018
This 4th Estate paperback edition 2019

1

A catalogue record for this book is available from the British Library

ISBN 978-0-00-830033-3

Printed and bound in Great Britain by
CPI Group (UK) Ltd, Croydon, CR0 4YY

Without the thought of death, it is impossible to make out anything in a human being. Its mystery hangs over everything.

SVETLANA ALEXIEVICH

The death of a loved one is actually also the death of a private, whole, personal and unique culture, with its own special language and its own secret, and it will never be again, nor will there be another like it.

DAVID GROSSMAN

For John
and our first grandson,
Manny

CONTENTS

PRELUDE

THIS IS A BOOK about the kinds of states that float somewhere between diagnosed madness and daily life. They are ordinary enough states and yet they are extraordinary. Without toppling us over into the register of specified mental illness, they can nonetheless hover close and scary. They are part of what make us individuals and not statistics, subjects for narrative, rather than objects for the sorts of studies that feed drug trials, corporations, advertising campaigns or state records. Humans are ample, often suffering beings. The machine model of cognition, of information processing, just isn't adequate to our complexity.

I am the principal 'case' in what follows, though really only a woman whose husband has recently died. His death launches me on a journey. It's not one that has an identifiable destination. Perhaps because of that the political and social atmosphere of the moment hover very close.

I have tried in the middle section of the book to investigate the ways in which our historical moment and the wider world could be understood as sharing a set of emotions with my own grieving state. Anger and loss are political, not simply personal feelings. They bleed into us collectively: the media and the social networks play their part. I have a hunch that the time we spend as and with 'disembodied' beings feeds into these dark feelings, too.

Sometimes they can be assuaged or at least counterbalanced by hope. Luckily that's where I landed in the final part of this book.

I hope my children will forgive my exposure. I have tried to be circumspect. Their mother is a reliable enough person, but when it comes to writing, the writer steps in.

GRIEVING

What I'm talking about now is a very ancient part of human awareness. It may even be what defines the human – although it [was] largely forgotten in the second half of the twentieth century. The dead are not abandoned. They are kept near physically. They are a presence. What you think you're looking at on that long road to the past is actually beside you where you stand.

JOHN BERGER

1

THE SMALL TRANSLUCENT bottle of shampoo outlived him. It was the kind you take home from hotels in distant places. For over a year it had sat on the shower shelf where he had left it. I looked at it every day.

I couldn't bring myself to move it or use it.

When I finally picked it up, it was caked and slightly clammy to the touch, like perspiring, not quite healthy skin. I put my glasses on to make out the indistinct print on the front of the curve. For the first time I could see that, next to the stylized palm tree, vanishing letters spelled out *Memory of Senses*.

I put the bottle back on the shelf. Quickly.

Though I had rid the house of bagsful of clothes, unopened packs of tobacco, wires that belonged to defunct machines, and some of the other random leavings of life, I somehow couldn't chuck that tiny bottle.

Superstition.

We all know the dead inhabit select objects. Even when we might also believe that they've gone to meet their maker or joined the elements in a field or river, or their everlasting souls have travelled up to Heaven to be judged by a supreme court at which angels bear witness to their deeds, good and bad, and eleven months of purgatory await.

Superstition: from the Latin 'over + stand'. A presence stands over us, one whom we fear or who might just bring us luck. Or perhaps, as in surveillance, that presence compounds security and fear. Cicero, that hoary old philosopher who, according to one of my school teachers, had intoned something about diseases of the mind being more common and more pernicious than those of the body, had considered the word to be a derivation of *superstitiosi* – literally those who are left over, the survivors or descendants. It is they who must perform the funeral rites for their dead. It is they who need superstition.

One of my superstitions as a performer of funeral rites seems to lie in a miniature bottle of shampoo, latterly found to bear the name *Memory of Senses*.

Had I unwittingly taken in that name well before noticing it? None of my senses had been behaving particularly well in the fourteen months, and rising, since he had died. My sight and hearing had all but abandoned the world. They were overrun, smothered by the assault from within. Maybe I had something in common with that other addled mourner, Hamlet, whose father's untimely death alongside his mother's way of grieving – curtailed too swiftly and sexually from his perspective as a son – sets up a fury in him that some term mad. He feels surveilled – by the state, by his father's ghost, and most of all by his own watchful, overwrought self.

2

DEATH HAD COME suddenly for John. It wasn't expected. Not by any of us. Even though he was undergoing an extreme new treatment, the details of which I can't seem to rehearse. Even though he had been in treatment for the first time just a little over two years before, then again in that last year. Twice. We had carried on laughing and arguing and walking and watching too many thrillers on the telly, and life didn't feel as if it were ebbing in any more definitive a way than usual. There was plenty of black humour and blunt speaking about mortality, but somehow these were jokes and quite unrelated to the real. On top of it all, he looked fit. Like himself.

So when the real came, it was utterly unexpected. A shock – like a wall toppling, knocking you down into rubble. Things smelt strange there, rot and ash. When you raised your head, skewed hallucinative vistas opened.

Part of the shock resided in the sheer corporeality of death. Nothing virtual there. The body turned to unresponding stone, massive, unforgiving, as it lay there on the raised bed in the intensive care unit. That unmoving body was more intractable than mere absence. It was stubbornly indomitable. It couldn't be wooed, or bargained with, or budged. Certainly not by me. Not over months of remembering. It was just there. A blunt fact. Somehow it was also a reprimand: how had we let him die?

We tend to think of dead bodies as abject in their lifelessness. I should have felt sorrow and pity. I had earlier while he was still breathing, but now – perhaps it was fear, or panic, or guilt, or all of them at once – his sheer stony immovability carried a visceral threat. Was it the latent violence of so much shiny steel and the high-tech tools that brought murder to my mind?

The evening before, I had had a loud panicking exchange with a bullying emergency-room doctor, who wanted to operate instantly: he just wouldn't listen when I said anyone from the cancer clinic would tell him that, given John's non-existent immune system, he couldn't be operated on. I was quietened by another doctor, and in the end, when the detail on John's file was read, no operation took place.

Had I been wrong? Was I complicit in the death? And did that mean, in the too many interpretations that accompany death, just as they accompany love, that I somehow wanted it?

He had lain there for a whole night before turning into stone. A night that stretched into infinity and gave way too soon, while the machines around him blipped and danced, with waves and reels of shining numbers. He still inhabited his body. He might not have been conscious, but we felt he was holding on beneath the closed eyes. Surely they would open again. His face wore a peaceful, benign expression, a counter-statement to the noise around him in that machine-crowded space.

When the children and their partners arrived, we all felt he could sense us, hear us. We stroked his forehead and, clustered round the bed, sang his favourites – Bob Dylan, Leonard Cohen, the Beatles, campfire songs. As if he were the fire. We talked to him one by one, too. I don't know what I said. I know there were tears – from the boys in particular. They were men returned to childhood by the death of a father, for one, a mentor, for the other. We willed him awake and simultaneously wanted to ease whatever passage there might be, if there was to be one. We hugged each other and him. No one quite knew who was holding whom up.

Around eight in the morning, the nurses had their rota shift and urged us all out for breakfast. We went obediently, sipped cappuccinos or double espressos with the office crowd at a Tottenham Court Road café. We talked inconsequentially. Or maybe it wasn't inconsequential. I don't really know.

We got back to the hospital in no time at all. But the room was uncannily quiet. The dancing screens had gone dark. A nurse I didn't recognize addressed me with a look that needed no words. He had used the opportunity. While we weren't looking, he had slipped away, like a dying animal seeking the shelter of the woods. Or perhaps they had just unplugged the machines that were functioning as his kidneys and other organs. Switched off the life-support. No life can be lived without support.

Now there was corporeality alone. A cooling body inelastic to the touch. Stony smooth. Both smaller and bigger than life, and accruing a spectral charge the longer I looked at it and held our daughter – though she might well have been holding me.

After that, time imploded. It was impossible to mark the sequence of days, of sleep and waking. It wasn't that, like W. H. Auden, I called out for the clocks to stop. They did so of their own volition. They stopped keeping time, moving the minutes and the hours, the days and eventually the months. Without their structure to cling to – a set of moorings so internalized we forget their existence – everything was cast adrift. There was no more continuity in my life, or rather in my self.*

---

* Some thinkers use the word 'trauma' to characterize such states, but since mine is an experience shared by everyone who has suffered loss, I prefer to limit this overused diagnostic term to more narrow and more extreme conditions.

3

MY FATHER HAD DIED in the same University College Hospital thirty-four years and three days before. I say 'the same', though in fact the old Victorian red-brick hospital no longer houses wards. The morgue on the lower-ground floor where I went to see my dad is now a lecture theatre.

Death had come for my father in the dank November when he entered his sixty-eighth year, old to me back then, though only two years older than my partner of thirty-two years, who seemed far too young to follow him.

I push away the image of my father at the last, cold and small in the great vaulted chamber that, in my memory, dwarfs everything inside it, though the figures – the prostrate one of my father, my mother bent over him – glow as if someone had turned a stage spotlight on them.

My mother is talking. She is whispering to my father, wrapping him in endearments, speaking Polish and Yiddish and French, though not English. I don't know why she is talking to him, since to us, her nearest family, it seemed he hadn't heard her for years and certainly can't now. Anyhow, I tell myself, she didn't love him – at least, not any more. They were always battling. She's not crying, I can see that. Where are her tears? Her keening? Her visible sorrow? Her words are empty and have no resonance.

I gaze at my father and know that just the evening before he had pleaded with me to get him out of there, out of the hospital. It was *me*, his daughter, he had asked – though in the delirium that took him back to the terror of the war years, I was his sister. He hadn't asked my mother: in his hallucination she was off cavorting with the SS guards.

Without realizing it, and because I probably preferred it that way, I took on the mantle of my father's wayward emotions. I didn't yet understand that the fragility that accompanies extreme illness, with the inevitable sense of diminishment it puts into play, often induces persecutory fear. Nearest to him, my mother had appeared complicit in his illness, so for him I was the loyal one, she the traitor.

That's why there are no tears in her wide blue eyes, I told myself, back then.

Through the lens of time, I recognize this as a daughter's narrative, one that comes with a propelling mythological force and is often replicated in ordinary families. The father-daughter bond is strong. Even where there's paternal jealousy of the line of suitors, the bond has none of the murderous or competitive charge of that between fathers and sons. Mothers are far more difficult for their daughters to come to inner terms with.

Athena, goddess of wisdom, never needed a mother at all and leaped fully formed from her father Zeus's brow. In Euripides' play, Electra urges her brother Orestes to murder their mother, Clytemnestra. She helps him push the sword down her throat, thereby avenging their mother's murder of their father, who had himself brutally sacrificed their sister – a fact Electra chooses to forget, at least until the deed is done. Antigone, at the end, leads her blind, ailing father Oedipus to Colonus. Freud, who reinvigorated the Oedipus story for modern times, called his own daughter, Anna, his Antigone. She became his voice and companion in older age, never betraying him with another man, often deprecating her mother, not only where intellectual matters were concerned.

We grow into our families and our myths simultaneously, the latter often enough shaped by the former, but the shaping also happens the other way round.

The mother-daughter bond is both trickier and stickier than the paternal one: daughters love their mothers but they need to leave them as far behind as Persephone did Demeter, descending even to Hell, to wriggle or leap somehow into independence and sexual awakening.

In adolescence, and often far beyond, it is imperative not to become the clone of that irritating, delimiting figure. The mother's ageing body – in Elena Ferrante's resonant *Neapolitan Quartet*, Lena's mother even has a telling limp – needs to be shed like a constricting skin and certainly barred from any associations with sex, even with Daddy. Yet we're glued to our mothers with that formative, largely wordless bond, which is a set of embodied gestures and rarely visible habits. She keeps coming back, smiling through our lips, lifting a hand to our hair, chiding the child we no longer are, but who is now another.

Back then, when my father died, I distrusted my mother. I was suspicious: she had never been able to give me a full medical history of my dad's ills (or hers, for that matter). I couldn't bear the thought that she harassed him for smoking. I would point out that she was killing him by forbidding him his killing cigarettes, so that he had secretly to wander the streets in search of them, losing his bearings in the process.

The daughter I then was treated her mother none too well. I couldn't fully embrace her. I questioned her judgement. I questioned the reality of her love for her husband of a lifetime. How was it that she could smile at a passing attendant, even while my father lay dead in front of her? Indeed, I colluded with my dying and delirious father's view of her: as we stood over him in the morgue, both terrified by the inert body between us, one of my few thoughts – or, rather, fantasies – was that perhaps if I had led him out of the hospital the previous evening, he would still be alive. Some part of me believed or wanted to believe there were hidden truths in his diabetic delirium.

After the visit to the morgue, I took my mother home. Once my brother had flown in, I left her in his hands. I convinced myself she preferred them. After the funeral, just a few days later, I went off to make love to a man I barely knew – as if enlaced bodies could save us from death's inertness.

Am I wiser, now that I have grown children of my own, about mothers and daughters, about the tug of unknown forces that lurches us into word or act or simply overwhelms and undoes us?

Perhaps. Perhaps not. Whatever the case, my children will inevitably see my blind spots and limitations. I know this, just as I know that I treasure them and they hold me dear. But knowing, though it helps, often can't save you from feeling, and the contradiction between the two, and everything it brings in train, can create a condition akin to madness.

I suspect we all experience it, just as we are all thrown into disarray by that other universal experience: death.

4

THIS IS NOT A ROMANTIC TALE. I would have liked it to be a story of adoring and honouring and tears of sadness over the great loss of a fine man. It is that, too, but it's not that alone. Death, like desire, tears you out of your recognizable self. It tears you apart. The eyes and arms, the recognition that used to hold you together as *you*, are no longer there. That *you* was all mixed up with the other. And both of those have disappeared. The I who speaks, like the I who tells this story, is no longer altogether reliable. Though now that I can begin to shape a sentence with that pronoun in it, I feel a little more like my old, if altered, self.

A day before he died, the morning after he had been moved into the fortress-like high-care hospital room from the cancer clinic next door, John uttered the words that resonated through me for months. Words can be performative.

We had been living for two weeks on the top floor of a building overlooking London's busy Tottenham Court Road, a three-minute walk from the shiny new clinic where the daily treatments took place. This was the hospital hotel. Each room had a patient and a partner or carer in it. There was a lounge and a breakfast-dining area. From one point of view, it was a tourist's delight – modern, clean, functional, central – but it was also a hellhole of illness and suffering. Everyone smiled, pretended cheer.

I was a star Pollyanna: though I'm a terrible and impatient nurse, I seem to be able to see the bright lining of most clouds, even thunderous ones. That night, I couldn't. It might have occurred to me then, or perhaps it was later, that no one at the hospital – in all respects a wonderful and pioneering institution – ever talked of death. They talked only of chances. We were gamblers in a high-tech casino, playing against unknown odds – unknown not only because of the newness of the treatment but because each body, let alone each mind and set of emotions, is so uncooperatively individual.

That evening, we had watched a DVD of some stand-ups and laughed uproariously. In the middle of the night, John fell over on his way to the bathroom some three metres from the bed. I was meant to take him to the clinic if that happened. Falling. It was a signal we had been warned of. He was in neutropenia – a pretty word used to describe a scary state of no immunity in which infections can rampage. It was four days after Day Zero – the apocalyptic name given to the day when the harvested stem cells had gone back into his chemically cleaned system. But the cells hadn't yet started their rebooting activity.

John flatly refused to leave the hotel room. He said he was fine and we would go in the morning. He was a man of considerable authority and stubbornness. I gave in without much argument. He did seem sort of fine now that he was in bed again. Rousing an emergency nurse might be worse than just sleeping. Or so I told myself.

In the clinic the following morning, we learned that an internal infection had set in. The nurse chided. A move into the multi-storey University College Hospital would follow imminently – or, rather, when a bed came free in the haematology ward with its sealed quarters. That only happened in the evening. With John in a wheelchair we were led along a subterranean passage through a block and a half of London streets. As the corridor twisted and turned, I wondered whether we were skirting the morgue where my father had lain.

Just like a thriller, I tried to joke.

Only as I write this does the body count my attempted joke may have conjured up for him come to me.

I waited until he was settled and asleep, then went to that now foreign place called home.

The next day was a Sunday. I drove to the hospital: it made it easier to bring food and fresh books. So focused was I on John getting better that I conveyed a week's worth. When I got to his room, he was asleep. Staff were busy elsewhere. There was no one of whom I could ask questions.

5

I AM SITTING on a plastic chair beside his bed. We are relatively high up, but the windows are murky and the light that comes in is grey and blemished. He is dozing, it seems peacefully. His lips are parched, and when he opens his eyes, I ask him if he'd like some water or some of the ice cream I've brought for him, thinking it might go down well. I've been inspired by the large number of lollies he was forced to eat while the harvested stem cells were introduced back into his blood with a drip.

He's weak and I feed him – just a few mouthfuls. He dozes off again, and sometime in that doze, he murmurs, 'I'm glad you're here.'

I stroke his hand. Tears come to my eyes. In all these gruelling weeks he has never before said that to me.

A little later he wakes again. This time he is more troubled. When the nurse comes to check on him, he grunts and groans. She has nothing to say to my questions, so I leave her to him, making my way through the two sets of doors that barricade the room from invisible killers. I stretch my legs. I realize that the dark is setting in. I also realize I haven't brought my specs with me and need them to drive in the dark. When I'm back with John, I explain I have to make a dash home. He tells me to take his pyjamas with me and wash them.

In the toilet the reek is overwhelming. I see a cascade of diarrhoea – in its midst sodden pyjama bottoms.

I come out and tell him there's no point. I'll bring fresh ones.

'No, take them,' he says. His eyes are two angry slits. 'Take them.' He raises his voice.

I know he loves these pyjamas above any others. They're ancient, but his favourites.

I go back into the toilet, not allowing myself to breathe, and realize I simply can't lift this squelch of body and other materials. I feel defiled. I will dissolve, liquefy into the stench. My body is turning to waste, mirroring his, yet I'm being called upon to be mother to this ageing toddler.

'That's all you're good for,' I hear him shouting. 'Cleaning shit.'

That was the last sentence he uttered to me. It hit me with the force of a body blow and mired me. Engulfed.

6

IF I RECOUNT such febrile unpleasantness, ordinary enough, it's because his words played themselves over and over in my ears and in my nose, night and day, after he died. When I was making coffee in the early hours of the morning, they clanged through my mind and filled the air. I would go to bed and they were there, waiting for me, with their attendant smell.

I was abased, worthless. A punished infant. Maybe it was the vertiginous throwback to helpless infancy that gave the words such power.

They set up one of the first refrains of my mourning state, punctuating my life for months of that year. Even when they had lost their stench, they seemed an ultimate judgement. The last words of the dying can be a terrible thing.

It's what he really thought of me, my inner voices say over and over. That was his final estimate. After all those thirty-two years together, that was what I was good for. Cleaning shit.

Of course I also realized that the fever was making him delirious. Of course I knew that a few hours before he had expressed a kindness, though I had now begun to doubt he had recognized the addressee of those words. Of course I knew he wasn't himself. But the cutting edge of the put-down, combined with the assault on the senses, reduced me to a cleaner of everyday detritus. The words seemed to have carved themselves into my flesh. Instead of Hester Prynne's A for adultery in Hawthorne's *The Scarlet Letter*, I wore an imaginary S.

Over the course of the next months, this judgement grew into the bottom line of our partnership and our afterthought of a marriage. In the scales of mourning, it weighed more heavily than our long years as lovers, partners, co-authors, intellectual sparring mates, devoted parents, friends. I was only good for cleaning shit.

As every novelist and reader knows, the end of a story colours everything that came before. I was shit-coloured.

Despite their far more evident delirium, I had half believed my father's last words to me about my mother, or at least the underlying truth of his fantasy. I had been pleased that he had mistaken me for a sister and taken me into his con-fidence. I hadn't considered for a moment what effect kindred words poured out to my mother might have had on her. Now I thought of her and her tearless state, her pleading voice as she addressed my father's dead body. Perhaps she, too, wanted some sign that their long lives together – in their case lived through the scarring turbulence of war as well as mundane peace – had had some value.

John's words took on the onus of his revenge on me for somehow staying alive, outliving him. They were my punish-ment, the sign of my guilt. They would toll in my ears every time anyone talked of him. They left me barely in control.

If a friend or an acquaintance sang his praises, spoke of his vast knowledge, his wit, his gentleness and kindness, I would instantly hear his last words and feel abased. I would want to fight back, fight out of this masochism and shout, 'Yes, kind to everyone, except to me!' I would have to struggle to thank friends and acquaintances offering warm condolences without somehow uttering a comment that put me in the frame as well, or drew attention to the fact that I might be valuable, too, that I was implicated in the good in his life.

I put a silencing lock on my lips, which were always in danger of betraying me. Never in front of the children, I repeated to myself, over and over, like a mantra. Honour, respect, admire, not this sullying narrative and the madness of my response.

But language was out of my control. I was out of control. It was impossible to do more than offer a smiling – or was it grimacing? – acknowledgement to reminiscences and consoling thoughts. Much as I might want to. Much as I appreciated the words and letters of friends and the person they almost conjured up, I couldn't trust my own lips – myself. The self I thought I knew, or at least had more than a passing acquaintance with, had gone missing.

Trapped in too many contradictions, I was in a perpetual rage in those first weeks and months, perhaps year. *Rage* – that ancient cornerstone of madness, so much one of its constitutive parts that in American English 'mad' is a cognate of 'angry'.

I couldn't read, certainly not fiction. Characters' names and doings would vanish as soon as my eyes had got to the end of a page, sometimes the end of a sentence. If I started a novel I wanted or needed to read, I could never get to the end. I just didn't want endings. The pile of novels by the bedside spilled over on to his side of the bed.

I couldn't trust my conversation with friends or children. I could just about watch television, though plot lines had preferably to be no more complex than Fred Astaire and Ginger Rogers could dance to: often enough, while they were dancing, his words and the reassessment of our conjoined lives they brought in their wake would return, and with it the racing anger. Eventually I graduated to *Colombo* and *The Good Wife*.

I am not normally an angry person. Quite the contrary. I don't hold resentments. I very rarely lose my temper. I occasionally shout at the news (more often in these recent years of alternative facts) but almost never, except during my children's teenage years, at anyone else. But here I was, raging all the time. Had I been bottling it up through those last years of illness?

Too late. The object of my rage was dead. Too soon.

It did occur to me, with a rare glimmer of light, that maybe death itself was my object. My rage would undo it, like those cartoon characters who propel their tiny swords into the fiery mouth of the dragon.

The march of fury with its rhythm of endlessly repeated questions – why did you? How could you? – kept him alive. It seemed he could occupy at least two states simultaneously. He could be the unpardoning, immovable granite body of his deathbed, and the absent presence with whom I argued ceaselessly in the hope that he would one day answer my questions and assuage my fury.

7

THE ANGER PROPELLED ACTIVITY. Ceaseless doing was the only escape from the flagellations of death, even though I couldn't altogether outrun them. I knew they would only stop if I succumbed to them utterly, lay down and allowed my own 'too, too solid flesh' to 'melt,/Thaw, and resolve itself into a dew!'.

Only when you're in the aftershock of death, do you realize quite how forensically Shakespeare charted that terrain. *Hamlet* is the great tragedy of states of mourning. Hamlet's melancholy and partial madness, his 'I am but mad north-north-west. When the wind is southerly, I know a hawk from a handsaw', his sexualized rage, his suicidal self-abasement; Ophelia's breakdown, her unhinged speech and suicide after Polonius's murder; even Gertrude's far too hasty leap into another bed, all spring from the lashings of death and the disturbances of grieving.

My body, which always seemed to know my wishes better than I did, had already opted for death at the end of John's first lymphoma treatment back at the start of 2014. It could do so again, surely, I now thought. That time I had just lain down on our bed after a dental appointment and woken up in an ambulance where my name was being çalled over and over. Somehow I couldn't reply.

All I recall of that cardiac arrest and briefly surfacing from some unknown depths is how wondrously pretty the paramedic was. I told her so, it seems, then passed out again to wake to the faces of my dear ones gathered round the hospital bed.

If he hadn't been at home that day, I would have gone first. Evidently some part of me wanted to go. Couldn't cope with the anxiety of his illness. Couldn't bear him dying. Couldn't bear the thought of an unanchored future in a land where, without him, I would once more feel intolerably foreign. Don't get me wrong. I enjoy my foreignness and the ethnographer's distance it affords. But too much tosses me back to the vertiginous childhood condition of being a migrant, who can't read the signs or tune into the language and with no place called home.

Better that I should have gone first, I now told myself over and over. I seemed to be in pain all the time in any case. My pills didn't agree with me and I kept passing out, so low was my heart rate. My inflammatory system went into overdrive, as if I had sustained injuries I had failed to notice. Was I mirroring what he had felt without complaint? My back, my shoulders, my head, my fingers, my chest, all the area around my heart ached. My body seemed to be indicating it was doing my dying for me and I should stop haring about.

A friend later told me that I seemed to spend all my time leaning on any surface available – the countertops in the kitchen, the back of a chair, the table – as if there was an unbearable weight in my body, in my bones, that I could not carry alone: 'like the heaviness that comes in dreams, that terrible inertia, that makes it impossible to run,' she wrote. I had Lethe-wards sunk, as Keats has it in his 'Ode to a Nightingale'.

Some die of heartbreak, the medics know too well. The eighteen months following the death of a partner seem to be precarious, particularly for women. So John Bowlby's study of mourning made clear back in the early 1960s.

The research shows that most women take a long time to get over the death of a husband and that, by whatever psychiatric standard they are judged, less than half are themselves again at the end of the first year. Almost always health suffers. Insomnia is near universal; headaches, anxiety, tension and fatigue are extremely common. In any mourner there is increased likelihood that one or more of a host of other symptoms will develop; even fatal illness is more common in the bereaved than it is in others of the same age and sex.

My mind might be absent, even as it chatted to friends who seemed to think I made sense, but it raced and sometimes my feet followed. The echoing family house, though it had been mine before he came into my life, was now rarely friendly. I kept walking from room to empty room, forgetting what I was looking for. I would rearrange flowers, plump up cushions, fold clothes for Oxfam, move books, papers, furniture. I think it was in those early days that I decided to shift the bed we had placed in the front room in case he was too weak to climb stairs when he got back from hospital. But that meant dislodging something else . . . and on it went. I was looking for an absence but that absence was also in myself. Neither of us could be found. Meanwhile there had to be the mutually contradictory acts of rearrangement and commemoration.

That I had been left to deal with bureaucracy, with the remains of too many days funnelled into an alien computer whose filing system made as much sense to me as a Rubik's Cube, was fuel for more rage and more activity.

Not that I can easily recall the particularity of most of my doings. I think I was living in a state of rational delusion. My scrappy, all-but-unreadable diary of the time is crowded with instructions to myself, meetings with family and friends, and crossings out. Pick up forms from hospital. Write to department in Cambridge. Sort out obits. See funeral director. Invite guests. Order flowers. Order funeral food. Contact Highgate Cemetery. Choose site. Confer with children. Write to banks. Find will. Speak to lawyers. Confer with children. Cancel, cancel, cancel. Fill out forms, fill out forms, fill out more forms.

The bureaucracy of death seems to want to compete with death itself in the horror stakes. I began to think it was winning.

At night and at odd times of the day I would pass into a state of torpid exhaustion and sleep the sleep of the dead uncluttered by dreams, or any dreams I can remember. Dreams or, rather, nightmares were daytime activities – at least initially.

One morning, I think it was just before the funeral, I came downstairs shivering. It was a dank, chill November, yet the house felt colder than usual. I wandered into the kitchen, turned the radio on for the sound of human voices, put the kettle to boil. A gust of cold air made me wrap my robe more tightly round myself. I followed the draught. It took me a few moments to realize that a window in the front of the house was open. A chill wind blasted through the room. How had I managed to leave that window open? I chastised myself for yet another random act of forgetting. I couldn't be trusted.

The stubborn window wouldn't close. It was always stiff, I reminded myself. Growing angry at my dwindling strength, I tried to position myself more strategically behind the sofa to heave down on the window frame. It was then my slippered foot arched awkwardly over some unseen object. I looked down and found a screw on the floor and beside it some chips of wood. Only then did my addled mind register that I hadn't been the one to leave the window open. It had been forced. I now saw a single broken lock on the floor, marks on the window frame where it had been jemmied up. An intruder. An attempted burglary. But he hadn't got in. The higher locks had held, and only a wraith or an infant could have squeezed through that foot of open space.

I poured coffee. My hand was shaking. It was him. I knew it. He was trying to come back. To come in. To break in. He should have asked. I would have unlocked the door.

Superstition. I knew I was being superstitious. I was also convinced. It was a sign. A portent.

I rang my son. He lived further away than my daughter, but he wasn't a reader of *Wuthering Heights*. He told me I had to call the police, at least to register the attempted break-in.

And to call our builder, ever a friend in need, who would come and fix the lock. I did all that, but I was nonetheless convinced that John was trying to break in, to come home. Whether it was because he missed me or wanted to chastise me – or both simultaneously – was the quandary.

8

FRIENDS WERE WONDERFUL through those days. They brought warmth and food. The fridge was piled high with delectables. We talked. We hugged. We drank a little. I don't know if they could see just how crazy I felt. I tried to smile. I was grateful to them. Grateful to my splendid children who came and sat, sometimes stayed, sometimes even had us all laughing at our ghosts.

Saturday, 5 December, the day of the funeral, dawned as grey and grim and cold as a funeral day proverbially must. The large chapel at Golders Green Crematorium was filled to capacity. I know who spoke. I had invited them. They were our nearest friends, John's closest colleague in Cambridge, his two brothers, the children and their partners, one of whom read a text sent by a dear mutual friend at Harvard, who couldn't be there. I know everyone spoke with eloquence and grace. They spoke with tenderness and, in the case of our daughter and son, with great courage. But I could concentrate on little that was said and remember next to nothing. Quite unlike the other occasions on which I have been in that chapel, when the well-chosen words of tributes resonated for weeks.

It was clear he was loved, admired, honoured. Whatever the noise in my head, I was pleased about that. Moved. I wanted to say a few brief words. Perhaps I wanted to say them in order to prove to him, to everyone, most of all to myself, that I was worth more than the lowly role to which I had been assigned.

The voice in my head, which had done much of the assigning, was punishing: it interpreted all this as a callow call for attention. A stupid self-aggrandizement.

Months later, I came across a passage from William James's *The Principles of Psychology* that made some sense of my overarching need for what convention might dictate as an unwifely visibility. James writes:

> No more fiendish punishment could be devised, were such a thing physically possible, than that one should be turned loose in society and remain absolutely unnoticed by all the members thereof . . . If every person we met 'cut us dead,' and acted as if we were non-existing things, a kind of rage and impotent despair would ere long well up in us, from which the cruellest bodily tortures would be a relief; for these would make us feel that, however bad might be our plight, we had not sunk to such a depth as to be unworthy of attention at all.

For some reason, on that occasion, the usual invisibility that attends the ageing woman's life felt akin to annihilation.

I talked for a brief moment about the John-shaped hole

in my life and read a poem by Adam Zagajewski that evoked
something of him, at least for me.

> Don't allow the lucid moment to dissolve.
> Let the radiant thought last in stillness
> though the page is almost filled and the flame flickers.
> We haven't risen yet to the level of ourselves.

I was facing him in the coffin as I read. I had the distinct
feeling that if he didn't like what I said he would sit up. I recall
being worried about any revealing verbal slips I might make.
I was frantic about the fact that he would soon be turned to
ash. Was ash worse than the stony implacable effigy he had
become in my mind? Or the phantom intruder? The night
before the funeral I had worked out that the day on which
he had uttered the words that had etched themselves into my
mind, like a festering scar, was *precisely* thirty-two years after
we had met.

Periodically, I would remind myself that his last words to
me were simply an indication that, like so many wives, I had
grown into my husband's mother: it is mostly mothers after all
who deal with babies' smelly mess. Freud's words in his essay
on 'The Theme of the Three Caskets', an essay John liked to
cite, often came to me: 'But it is in vain that an old man yearns
for the love of woman as he had it first from his mother; the
third of the Fates alone, the silent Goddess of Death, will take
him into her arms.'

The human condition doesn't really help all that much
when one is being all too human. I had thought, once the

funeral was over, I would be less crazy, less alert to the perpetual babble of those inner voices, less susceptible to rage,
those racing, chattering demons in my mind, that were so hard
to outrun. The Furies, the ancients called them.

I wasn't. I shouldn't have let the need for activity take me to
his desk.

IT MUST HAVE BEEN a few days before the funeral. I needed
to find his will so that all the formal matters of death and the
state could be sent on their way. He had told me it was in his
desk.

I had never particularly liked that desk, heavy and stolid
and post-war, but he was attached to it. It had belonged to his
father. In all our years together I had rarely looked inside it and
then only under instruction about where and for what.

I started to rifle round. I realized I was nervous. I may have
written the occasional thriller, but outside books, I have a deep
sense of privacy. Or at least I do in the normal course of things.
I never rifled through my children's diaries, and though I once
read some letters I had found in the back of a cupboard that
turned out to have been from an early girlfriend to my son, I
felt ashamed doing it, as if I had turned into my own mother, a
constant rifler. Or maybe, much as I want to know, I'm simultaneously frightened of finding things out, as if a trap lies at the
end of every dark, twisting corridor.

He must have known that, since I didn't need to do much
rummaging. The first thing my eyes fell on in the very top
drawer was an envelope full of photographs. I love photos.
I picked it up, looking forward to a break from the duty of

locating a will. The anticipated baby pictures didn't materialize. These images were of a woman in a variety of fetching poses and smiling to the camera or the person holding it in the way one smiles only to intimates. I knew that woman. I knew that photographer.

I sat back and tried to take a deep breath. It caught on something. Maybe it was fury. The kind you can't swallow. The kind that doesn't let you breathe. I now started to look in earnest, pushing things aside, prodding, hating what I found, hating myself, hating him. I opened his wardrobe and started to heave out his clothes.

Some nine years before, we had split up. He was in the midst of what can only be called a mid-life crisis and passionate about a young woman. He was also crazy, crazier than any adolescent in the grip of lust and jealousy. Undone by it. The part of me that writes understood. This was another form of everyday madness, more familiar than so many others. He was a man obsessed.

I would have been prepared to tolerate a short burst of passion, but not the palpably self-destructive process he was engaged in and the harm it occasioned all round. In any event, the last person he wanted near him was me, with my Cassandra-like predictions, my world-weary plaints that made his trajectory more mundane than mud. Or comical, like a door slammed in a farce.

The abandonment so late in our coupled lives undid me. A hot, jealous fury attended my days, shrivelling everything in its wake, like a mountain fire. The only way I could seem to deal with the tearing apart of my life and the detritus it left behind was to throw myself into more and other ways. I was already active in English PEN: I took on the presidency. I became chair of the Freud Museum. I got *Mad, Bad and Sad* ready for publication. I found myself devising and editing a new series on 'Big Ideas' for Profile Books. On and on it went.

The rage and the need for distraction from it that attended the first parting of our ways was close kin to my mourning state, a kind of trial run of the emotions. Now, after his death, one historical moment collapsed into another. That second dismantling echoed the first. Pain always leaves deeper traces in memory than pleasure – and I was plunged back into an old, intolerable pain. I hated him and hated myself. Bits of myself and my past had to be torn out, emptied of their destructive charge and somehow sewn back in so that I could walk and run and speak as a functioning person, let alone love and still have a history.

Within both states I felt as mad and sad to myself as some of the historical figures that had peopled my books on the subject. If I didn't quite make it to the condition of the 'bad', it's only because I wasn't altogether certifiable. The racing thoughts, the compulsions, the sudden mental absences or holes in time when I would find myself walking on a street I hadn't set out for, these were just everyday madness inflected by loss and by grief. As long as I could get up in the morning and make a semblance of working or arranging the flowers and objects in the house, as long as the children were there, as long as I had to put on a face to greet them and to meet the faces I met, I would manage, manage it, manage myself.

The difference between the terrors of the first abandonment and the second was that after the first I could rail with friends about men's antics and a woman's lot. Now, there was only one person I could even begin to talk to, and then only sporadically. Back then, after a little less than a year, John pleaded that he wanted to return to his life, our life together. After a month of persuasion, I agreed. Many of my friends disapproved of what looked like my moral laxity, my lack of feminist firmness. But I preferred to be coupled, preferred my children to have their father in place. I like the familiar. I liked to have someone there to discuss days and ways and news with, to feel grounded. It was hard to laugh on one's own. I liked to laugh. I liked ordinary life.

Already back then, I had a deep sense of the ways in which that ordinariness is so readily traversed by madness. We may be rational creatures, deeply individual, but loss illuminates just how readily the ever-uncertain fortress of reason crumbles, and how fundamentally our individuality is made up of our attachments to others.

One of the differences in the separation that mourning constitutes, apart from the major one of irreversibility, was that I wasn't sanctioned from the outside to hate, to be angry. Composure was required; so was admiration of the lost one. And I had others to care for. Impossible for me to take on the capacious mantle of the vibrant Wife of Bath, who had buried six husbands. Or become one of those widows of whom Wilde's Lady Bracknell could say, 'I hear her hair has turned quite gold from grief.' Or the amorous Merry Widow who gave her name to various bits of saucy lingerie. After all, I didn't only hate.

I was caught in ambivalence, perhaps a deeper plight than the now fashionable term 'cognitive dissonance', which highlights the trap of feuding ideas, but not that of warring emotions, the kind that probably have deep roots in a time when language wasn't to hand to make sense of things.

I was terrified that the other woman, any other woman, would turn up at the funeral. I suddenly had an acute sense of why Greek rites incorporated professional mourners – those women who, like so many Maenads, tore at their hair, wailed and keened to the elements, their dirges abstract public rituals. Part of me would have wanted to join them, or wholly to give mourning over to others.

But there were too many parts of me.

9

AFTER I HAD FOUND that first set of photos, I would creep into John's study regularly. Sometimes his phantom stood over me as I plundered his desk and possessions for more signs of betrayal. He hadn't been true to his word – he had never been true. The jealous thoughts spiralled, took wing, raced through Heaven (his) and Hell (mine) and I grew smaller and smaller, a bit of rag and bone in the gleaming arcade of his life. I scoured his obtuse computer for tell-tale emails. His diaries, ranked in a desk drawer like so many tin soldiers awaiting amorous campaigns, refused to give up any more than the signs of daily institutional battles. I looked for code. When had he last seen her, or any of the others? He had always been far more attached to his lost and dead, his past, than his present. I knew that. I had neither left nor died. I found ample documents from that past, his past – photos, letters, huge hordes of them when we all went to begin to clear his Cambridge office. He kept everything.

The children thought I had just grown weak and grumpy from the dust, the monumental task of confronting his remains and the effort of removal. There was more. My mind was askew. It became clearer and clearer to me that I was the only one of whom there was no trace. I was nowhere in his life. Not in the life that he wanted to *keep*. To store against the forces of time. In our scores of family photos and holiday pics, there were so few of us together. There were fewer letters, not on paper. I didn't exist either in the historical archive or in his imagination. I was just the daily help. Cleaner of excrement.

An analyst friend, underlining that this wasn't very analytic but analysis wasn't what I needed, advised me that as soon as I found my thoughts going off in this obsessive direction, I should think about something, anything else – groceries, the grandchildren, the garden, the tasks ahead, German verbs . . . A self-fashioned cognitive behaviour therapy or simply a form of diversion.

The founder of alienism, the great Philippe or Citizen Pinel, known as the liberator of the insane, leaped into my mind. He practised 'distraction' with patients who were perfectly lucid and reasonable except for *idées fixes* that had established themselves in one given area of their reasoning. Napoleon, for example, might be a trigger point. With people who suffered from oppressive passions – among which Pinel lists hatred, jealousy, remorse and, of course, grief – theatrical ruses might help, or stays away from home. Distraction, it seemed, was palliative; so were holidays.

But none of it helped quite enough. Only time would do that, and not yet, perhaps never completely. This wasn't a bout of flu that could be got over and put behind one with minimal fuss.

Hard to admit, but my frenzy of searching, both physical and mental, had a distinct sexual charge. I no longer or only rarely saw John on his deathbed, or even as he had been through those long arduous years of treatment. He had grown younger. His hair had darkened and there was more of it. He had become the man I had first met more than three decades before.

It took a while, but I eventually realized that all my racing internal arguments with him – how could you? Why did you? Why aren't you? Don't you love me? Why did you bother coming back to our conjoined lives? Why? When? How? – all these howling questions, with their component of desire and jealousy, love and hate, were a vigorous attempt to bring him back. In the flesh.

If he were back, then I could scream and he could answer my questions. I could rant at his perfidy. I could unleash my resentment. I could kill him. And we could make up.

In Proust's *À la recherche du temps perdu*, after Marcel's lover Albertine has died, he writes:

My jealous curiosity as to what Albertine might have done was unbounded. I suborned any number of women from whom I learned nothing. If this curiosity was so tenacious, it was because people do not die for us immediately, but remain bathed in a sort of aura of life which bears no relation to true immortality but through which they continue to occupy our thoughts in the same way as when they were alive. It is as though they were traveling abroad.

I preferred John to be travelling abroad, to remain in the realms of desire.

To be desired, my old friend John Berger writes, is perhaps the closest anybody in this life can reach to feeling immortal.

I would have preferred to have John immortal and doubtless have a little of that immortality myself. Instead all I had was a half-empty shampoo bottle. *Memory of Senses*.

When I looked up the word 'bereavement' in the *Oxford English Dictionary*, it turned out to be etymologically linked to the old Germanic 'reave' – to plunder by force, to carry out raids in order to rob. I felt plundered. Be-Reft. My partner was gone. My lived past, which had been lived as a double act, had been ransacked, stolen. The story of my own life had to be rewritten. And I was guilty. Guilty of being a survivor. Literally. Before the late 1960s turned people like my parents – who had, against all the odds, made it through the war – into survivors, a survivor was simply someone who outlived another.

10

In one of his seminal insights, Freud linked the state of mourning to the condition of melancholia, which we would now call depression. The characteristics that mourning shared with depression include

> a profoundly painful dejection, a cessation of
> interest in the outside world, loss of the capacity to
> love, inhibition of all activity, a lowering of the self-
> regarding feelings to a degree that finds utterance in
> self-reproaches and self-revilings, and culminates
> in a delusional expectation of punishment –

The singular difference is that in mourning 'the lack of interest and turning away of activity' common to depression has an exception when it comes to that connected with 'thoughts of him'.

Both states are set in motion by loss.

In one of his understated asides, Freud notes, 'It is really only because we know so well how to explain it that this attitude [in mourning] does not seem to us pathological.' This is particularly the case if one considers that a clinging to the dead through the medium of a 'hallucinatory wishful psychosis' can be part of mourning, too.

In his 'Thoughts on War and Death' written in 1915, very soon after *Mourning and Melancholia*, he elaborated the inevitable ambivalence that unwittingly characterizes all our loves:

> These loved ones are on the one hand an inner
> possession, components of our own ego; but on the
> other hand they are partly strangers, even enemies.
> With the exception of only a very few situations, there
> adheres to the tenderest and most intimate of our
> love-relations a small portion of hostility.

This small portion of hostility can quite easily grow large in the dead partner with whom we in part identify, just as children identify with their parents, take them in, often enough later on only to spit them out. It is these very parts in the other that then turn back on us rampantly, like an avenging conscience, to persecute us into abjection once they have been lost. Have gone.

The French psychoanalyst Jacques Lacan talked about such cruel and vindictive self-persecution as the work of an 'obscene super-ego', the super-ego being in Freudian terms that internalized, endlessly repetitive, sadistic and rancorous conscience – initially shaped out of our parents' prohibitions and cultural settlements on good and bad – that yaps away at us like a small-town bully, belittling us, turning us into a nether likeness of Hamlet, one without poetry. In a wonderful riff on self-criticism, the analyst Adam Phillips evokes a Hamlet whose dangerous desire for vengeful murder is converted into a form of character assassination – his own: 'the character assassination of everyday life, whereby we continually, if unconsciously, mutilate and deform our own character'.

The Hungarian-born Melanie Klein, so influential in understandings of psychoanalysis in Britain, thought of mourning as a reactivation of the inevitable early-childhood depression: the loss of the loved person, like the loss of internal 'good objects' in infancy, threatens a collapse. Mourning is thus a maddening process in which hatred, guilt and love oscillate until the 'internal good objects' can be reinstated and the dead person put to rest.

And all of this while we're having a cup of coffee with a friend and talking about the weather. Stormy in these days of inner warming. Holding out hope, too, that those internal good objects come round.

Not that there's a mother in sight anywhere.

11

THE WOMAN WHO is a simulacrum of me and not a dishev-elled midnight gorgon, punished from all sides and punishing in turn, goes about her duties. She tries to be a good mother and grandmother; she deals with the bureaucracy of death and the lawyers who are its servants; she tries to concentrate on the minutiae of pensions and old share certificates more abstruse than incunabula. She writes bits – an artist's catalogue preface, an essay for the BBC. She sits at a desk and finishes the book he hadn't quite finished. She prepares the second for publi-cation. She hunts for an archive for his work. She puts in train memorials and conferences. At these she manages more or less to utter a few lucid sequential sentences. Or at least she thinks she has for a moment, before going home to beat herself up.

The reality was that I could work on 'thoughts connected to him', as Freud called them, but not on much else for long spans consecutively. Not only had I been his first reader and editor for years, but the work allowed me to focus, more or less, on the public portions of him. The positive side effect was that I was able to concentrate on the parts of him I wasn't so preoccupied with hating. This activity was, I imagine, an attempt to repair the destruction I had wrought on him and he on me.

Though I was still alive.

I wasn't an altogether good enough mother, though. My daughter admonished me for being short-tempered with her and not sufficiently sensitive to her own grieving or, on one or two occasions, for erupting in negative asides about her beloved dad. I didn't mean to. I wasn't always aware that I had. But I evidently had. All this made me think about my own mother all those years ago after my father had died. I really did need to consider the generational cascade of repetitions or hauntings that are an all but inevitable part of family life.

My mother's own display of tears had been confined, as far as I witnessed, to the deathbed. After that she had smiled in her usual sunny way through thick and thin and stayed cool, while I tumbled as rapidly as I could into bed with a man, as if to confirm the eternal strife between death and life.

Given that I had read so many novels in which families fall asunder as soon as the patriarch dies, his departure igniting siblings and their children to war, let alone newer and older wives, I had little excuse for straying into the trap of bickering and conflict with my own brood. But my inner madness came in unpredictable waves and sometimes bubbled over and out. The smiling coolness my daughter sometimes wondered at was the mirror image of my mother's; the harsh wartime survival stories she told, in which my father appeared diminished, were perhaps the equivalent of my negative asides.

As I had for my own mother, my daughter often thought she knew what was best for me. I, too, had known better than my mother about the ways of the contemporary world and, in my assumptions of knowing, had been even more emphatic than my wonderful daughter. But I balked when it came to me. Though I obediently trailed off to see doctors when ordered to, made sure there was food in the fridge, and invited friends over one at a time, I also sensed that, just as I had, my daughter needed me at important points to maintain my maternal authority. Then, too, I wasn't altogether ready for a full King Lear reversal. Yet at times, for the first six months after her father's death, I seriously considered it. Giving in and giving up seemed very seductive.

I knew my daughter was suffering at the loss of her beloved dad, who had adored her in turn. I also knew that the loss had come at a particularly difficult time for her. His advice and towering pride in her would have been important. My occasional irritability or inappropriate babble was in some instances the mask of control slipping. Early in that first year, though it might already have been summer, and after a difficult lunch, I emailed her:

> I'm sorry if I haven't been paying enough attention to the ups and downs of grieving.
>
> I find the process utterly unpredictable, like a deep rumble inside one which sums up all the lacks there have ever been, and isn't really assuageable. Sometimes it's too loud to hear anything else. So I kick against it. At other times it's just there, a dull throb, a backdrop that you don't have to confront, and I race along in my deaf way. I will try to be more sensitive to you.

Needless to say, I don't remember the precise situation that necessitated this apology.

I THOUGHT OF MY MOTHER a lot in those days and nights of an afterlife in which I was battling for some kind of clarity. Her husband had died in a country she barely knew. They had only recently retired and made a home here. She had few friends of her own, but she tried to make do. She flew to and from Canada, where my brother and his family lived. She was a little lost now in both countries. Her often irascible daughter (me) had recently split up with her husband, and had a small child with whom Granny had a deep bond. That, I now realize, is probably what in large part kept her coming here and led her to spend more time in London.

She took in a lodger who was a friend of mine. He happened to be black: she had no idea that neighbours' lips would curl and malicious chatter would erupt among visiting friends from abroad. She rarely talked of my father. Perhaps she felt not unlike I have in the aftermath, but it wasn't something she could talk about or perhaps accede to. The very thought of madness, even of the everyday kind, would for her have carried a stigma. And she was proud.

When she died, purportedly of a cold, twenty years later, after two final years of Alzheimer's had robbed her of English, French, and all recognition of her nearest, I found a few of my father's things still in her house. A silk robe, some cufflinks, an ancient prayer shawl, rarely worn, that might well have originated before the Second World War in Poland and made its way with them through their various migrations. She still wore her wedding band. Before that last long illness took a grip on her, when she talked of my father it was always of him as a younger man, even if that brought memories of terrible times. More often, as she grew older, her own father and brother captured her attention, earlier losses that had deeply affected her. It seems one loss reinvigorates all the prior ones. Death is most at home with other deaths.

It's shaming to admit, but I didn't mourn her death. Her mind had left her body behind several gruelling years back, and her ultimate passing felt like a relief to everyone. Only years later did I begin to dream about her and allow her to inhabit my life once more. She would often appear with a calm, youthful smile in the kind of rural landscape I didn't consciously associate with her, as if some part of me wanted her to be returned to a girlish innocence.

12

WE BURIED JOHN'S ASHES on 19 February 2016. It was a bitterly cold grey day. We planted a rose bush for him that would eventually burst with dark pink buds for the length of the summer, and surrounded him with anemones and primroses. He loved flowers, he loved digging, was a keen gardener. We read – psalms, poems, Raymond Carver's 'Late Fragment', which always brings tears to my eyes, even when I'm not crying. It formed part of my ongoing inner conversation with John. I had met Carver once and remembered him as a big gentle bear of a man, though I certainly knew he wasn't only that.

> And did you get what
> you wanted from this life, even so?
> I did.
> And what did you want?
> To call myself beloved, to feel myself
> beloved on the earth.

Putting John in the ground in a carefully chosen and beautiful spot at the top of a hill, not far from George Eliot, Karl

Marx and Eric Hobsbawm, a friend who had also known John's father, seemed not only crucial but an important marker. I selected the site with an eye to the fact that it was overseen by a stone angel. As importantly, we could push through brambles and stand on a ledge to see the grave from Waterlow Park, where long ago we used to take the children for walks. I thought once we had buried him on this familiar hill close to so many friends, my mind would be easier and his ghost calmer.

There was still a distance to travel, one full of potholes you could tumble into and never surface from again, without somehow acquiring a new, transformed shape.

One day, on my way home from a meeting in the Strand, I did literally tumble. It must have been April, by then. I was feeling just a little pleased with myself for having performed adequately, not fainted, managed sanity, or what passes for it, and even humour. Then, by some aberration, I decided to run for an approaching bus. I never take the bus. I hadn't run for years. But I ran then along a crowded Aldwych, weaving between people, like some ancient rugby player toting a bright blue bag instead of a ball. The pavement wasn't impressed. The ground under my feet rebelled. I fell flat on my face. A crowd gathered round. The pain, the shock, the humiliation were dreadful, but by some miracle, I hadn't broken anything, not even, it turned out, my nose, though it felt distinctly out of joint. A nice young woman put me into a cab. By the time I got home my face had started to turn black and blue. The next morning, I looked like a victim of serious domestic abuse. The trouble was, I was my own domesticity.

And even then, in the midst of terrible pain, the tears didn't come.

Nor would the ground quite hold John. A furry new revenant, a bear-like charcoal cat, silky to the touch, with a round face and intent yellow eyes, appeared. We had seen it here and there on the street for several years. I think he was a British shorthair. John had a fondness for him. Now the cat decided he really needed to move in with me. No sooner was the front door open than he would streak past and disappear into the house. I would look diligently in every room and under sofas. Invariably I would find him upstairs, curled up in pride of place on a plush red velvet armchair in John's study, right next to his desk. I began to think he looked a little like the chair's last incumbent. Had John been transformed into this unreadable familiar? I would carry Puss out, not wanting to leave him in the house alone. But I felt as guilty as if I were putting John, himself, out.

IN MAY, almost exactly six months after John had died, we held a memorial in Cambridge. A great deal of planning had gone into the event, not only by myself: his departmental administrator was key.

I had been looking forward to this ritual moment. Surely this would shift things, I told myself. The obsessive inner monologue would abate, the rage, the superstitions. I would no longer be quite so susceptible to the waves of grieving madness.

But I feared the event simultaneously. Universities are rarely altogether hospitable to those outsiders called partners.

Close friends of ours had gathered from abroad, from America and Germany and France. His department, History and Philosophy of Science, of which he had been head for years, convened a day for students, former students and colleagues. A public memorial in the beautiful Great Hall at his college, King's, followed, and finally drinks at the Whipple Museum of Science, which the department houses.

One-time students, colleagues and friends evoked a person I must also have known, since I had known John well, known his dedication, the breadth of his knowledge, his humour. Yet my mind kept wandering as soon as anything personal was mentioned, as if the only plot I could follow was the purely intellectual one. Everyone gave the impression of intimacy.

Neither did I always recognize the man evoked – had I so remade his image in myself that he could no longer be remembered, reassembled, reconstituted as other, outside myself? I struggled to recall half of the incidents at which I was purportedly present. I struggled to thank people graciously, even though I was so very grateful to them. I simply struggled. Remembering, putting the body and mind parts together again, seemed once more, and despite the passage of time, to reinvigorate shock and hostility. Only the Bach at the end of the proceedings, played by the talented Kryszia Osostowicz – the Sarabande in D from Partita No. 2, followed by the Largo in F Major from Sonata No. 3 – seemed to knit together ragged threads and provide peace. And the embrace of friends.

13

FROM THE OUTSIDE, she must seem like a thoroughly admirable, certainly a good enough widow, I thought consoling myself, after the memorial, about this other, often angry, person who was also me. Look how fittingly the memorial went. And look how hard she's working not to die immediately even though she wants to; look how she's struggling to make things right for her children and grandchildren so they won't have to wade through tons of mess now or after she's gone. Doesn't she realize that they probably will, whatever she does?

A good enough widow.

I realized I hated the word. It was a box that might sport a small window, but it was very close to a coffin.

All those literary widows whom publishers and biographers feared and loathed came to mind, the ones who traditionally guarded the estates of their far greater (and often far older) husbands, like fiery dragons. With their children or executors, they burned letters and diaries, and were reviled for adulterating the historic record. Not that I shared their status, either social or historical, but I understood their need to control. Without those gestures towards order, towards keeping the dead in their preferred image, they themselves might easily tumble into visible madness, the tearing out of hair and shredding of clothes.

I was a contemporary independent woman. I had never – in the way of women and widows before the Married Woman's Property Act of 1870 – been the legal property of my husband, a *femme co(u)verte*, turning over my identity and my earnings to him, depending solely on him and unable to recoup what might initially have been mine even after his death. No. Laws and customs had changed, but the word 'widow' still contained a whiff of sulphur, particularly if you weren't young enough to be merry.

I could now definitely see the attraction of hoisting papers into the fire and not having to sort and sift, let alone finding or keeping for posterity what was best forgotten. If I hadn't yet considered jumping into a pyre, practising suttee or sati, like those good Hindu wives of yore ('good wife' being what the word means), who purportedly thought of themselves as part of their husbands and certainly had no independent legal life or means, it's because flames are not the way I want to go.

The word 'widow' comes from the Indo-European word *widhewo* married to the Latin *vide*, all of which means 'to be empty, separated or destitute'. It's one of the few words in which the basic form applies to women, the suffix 'er' being necessary to specify the male. If this is because men on the whole have not, either historically or today, stayed widowers for very long, the dictionaries don't say. In John Bowlby's classic study of mourning, which focused on the bereaved aged forty-five or younger, 50 per cent of men in the statistical cohort of 700 had remarried or were about to after a year or less of mourning. The women took very much longer to re-couple, if at all.

The archaic 'viduity', meaning widowhood, chimes with *vide* or 'empty', suggesting lack and want. In Samuel Beckett's *Krapp's Last Tape*, the gloomy old protagonist, trapped in never-ending repetition, hears the word in an early tape of himself he is replaying:

> Back on the year that is gone, with what I hope
> is perhaps a glint of the old eye to come, there is
> of course the house on the canal where mother lay
> a-dying, in the late autumn, after her long viduity.

He starts, plays the section again and, murmuring the word, goes off in search of a dictionary from which he reads a long definition that puzzles, then amuses him. Is it the word itself, the fact that he no longer quite recognizes it, or that his mother is at last off to join his father that gives Krapp momentary pleasure?

Sylvia Plath's devastating poem 'Widow' has a near-Gothic resonance – 'widow' is a word that consumes itself, a dead syllable with a shadow of an echo, a 'great, vacant estate!'. Daddy's idealizing daughter, Plath was her mother Aurelia's alone from the age of eight. It was a relationship fraught with difficulty. Plath rarely manifested her deeper thoughts to her mother. She enacted them in suicide attempts instead. Aurelia outlived her by thirty-one years, a terrible fate for both. The widow wears death as a dress, Plath writes.

Freud uses the word 'widow' only three times in all the twenty-three volumes of his work in English. It was the loss of the father that spurred his thinking and his seminal *The Interpretation of Dreams*; and later, like Darwin, the terrible loss of a daughter. Darwin and his wife Emma treasured a box full of their little Anna's keepsakes – discovered at their home, Down House, long after their deaths. Freud, who stoically eschewed sentiment, nonetheless made one of his great discoveries about absence and how it can be contained and mastered by repetition through his daughter Sophie's son, Ernst, and his game of 'fort/da' – Gone and Here. This consisted of the child throwing a spool on a string out of his cot and retrieving it while uttering the words: the child's ability to control the going and coming of his toy transformed an unhappy situation – parental absence – into a manageable one through a repeated game. If at the time eighteen-month-old Ernst played this game, his mother was not yet permanently gone, when Freud published *Beyond the Pleasure Principle*, she was.

Some might speculate that Freud's resistance to thinking directly about the condition of those left behind by their spouses is not unlinked to the fact that his own, rather demanding, mother outlived his father by thirty-four years and died only nine before her eldest son. Widows, female or male, don't even come into *The Psychopathology of Everyday Life* where you'd imagine they'd be rampant. But, then, widows are scary people – or scared people, which may not always be far from the first.

Freud's first use of the word 'widow' is in relation to anxiety caused by abstinence, the second in the context of a taboo among many native peoples against consorting with the dead. Illness and death seem to be contagious, so the prohibitions stretch to widows and widowers. In some places, the very presence of people who have been close to the dead is considered unlucky, and may indeed kill those who lay eyes, certainly hands, upon her or him. Lurking behind such practices, and the sense of threat surrounding the widow, Freud suggests, is the danger of *temptation*. Widows and widowers must 'resist a desire to find a substitute' for their partner too quickly or 'arouse the desire' in others. This runs counter to the sense of mourning and kindles the ghost's wrath.

Freud's late nineteenth-century ethnographic sources may not be as far away as we think. Certainly the continuing power of *Hamlet*, of Gertrude's 'unseemly haste' overlaps with such understandings. So did my occasional early forays into society outside the ritual circumstances of funerals or memorials. These had a comic side. Apart from your nearest friends, people avoid you. You may resent it, but in fact you want to be avoided. You would avoid yourself, if you could. After all, you're inhabited not only by the other, but by death.

In crowded rooms, the occasional book events I needed to go to, the acquaintances who knew of my 'bereavement' mostly preferred to move out of eye contact or, if they came close enough for conversation, felt they needed to talk about John, whom I was trying to escape. In the earliest months, I struggled to refrain from interposing negative comments, or exposing my desire for retaliation, which was also my fear of his. I let their stream of words wash over me as if they might wash me clean.

Or we assiduously and awkwardly avoided the elephant in the room.

When people did talk about John, remember an incident, or a time of their lives when they had been close to him, it always seemed to me they felt they knew him better than I did. Perhaps they did. Certainly at that moment, in evoking him, they knew him better. I tried to hoard what they said in the hope that at some point I would re-idealize him, but their words rarely found solid enough ground to be implanted and were washed away by that night's waves of rampant emotion.

For those who didn't know of John's death, the opening gambit of 'How are you?' became a wonderful charade worthy of John Cleese in the ongoing theatre of English embarrassment. If I said, 'Fine', I was lying, and inevitably at some point in any conversation, the truth would tumble out, and flushed faces and apologies on both sides would follow. In any event, in those first months sustaining a conversation with more than one or a maximum of two old friends at a time was all but impossible. That got easier. By the time the first bulbs had shown themselves, I was able to have more than a single person to dinner and somehow manage the food, the conversation, and sometimes even his domain – the wine – as if I weren't half a being struggling to keep my head above unfriendly waters. But apart from my closest, I continued for a while, at least, to find strangers far easier. I guess you can build a different, separate self through unknown eyes.

The corporate sector is better prepared for widows. I put through many phone calls to unknowns in that first year. If I explained that the matter was connected to my late husband, voices would change. Glaswegian would turn into a close cousin of received English. Essex twangs would metamorphose into a version of the Church of England pulpit. The Irish, ever pleasant, would grow in slowness and consonants. Everyone was transformed into a vicar. I had a vision of an erstwhile priest providing bereavement training for banks, pension and other funds, transforming idiolects into the best condolence voices and providing perfect patter. 'We are sorry for your loss,' the voice would confide, before turning me over to a 'bereavement service', where I was treated with far more telephonic respect, not to mention patience, just in case I lost my rag, than I have ever experienced. The patterns were strictly laid down and almost always avoided the word 'death'.

The Counselling Directory for Bereavement has a sensible description of mourning giving it four stages, not quite the Alcoholics Anonymous twelve-step plan, and there's no promise of godly power to hold you up and help you along. It begins by telling you that 'Grief can shake everything up – your beliefs, your personality and even your sense of reality,' and it stresses that manifestations of grief are individual: there are no wrong or right ways. It can also last longer than the year Freud had initially determined as the dividing line marking the difference between mourning, that ordinary if extraordinary part of common life, and the condition of depression. All of which is very consoling, as are the vicar-like corporates on the telephone.

They don't, of course, stop you feeling deranged – from being certain you've spotted him on the other side of a crowded room, or standing in the tube: yes, only he had that lack of neck, that wrinkle of suit and tell-tale crease at the shoulders.

Or holding on just a fraction too long when saying goodbye to a relative stranger, who happens to have some assemblage of girth and size that feels oddly familiar.

Nor do they help you get to grips with what can be experienced as an *interminable* (but please don't terminate!) period of illness, a.k.a. treatment. This is a common experience of contemporary life, certainly in the West. During what can well be years in the stranglehold of unstoppable anxiety and hospital-led lives, coupledom frays. Personalities and settled or unsettled power (im)balances take on new inflections. Symptoms float and are shared. Resentments form and are buried to surface at odd times. Patience and compassion are taxed on both sides of the couple, ill and illest, and indeed in the family as a whole, as good children try not to wish their parents dead or at least hold on to an image of them that is tolerable.

There is little escape from the daily toil and toll of this prison from which there is no exit but death; it brings its own punishment for the unspoken wish. Nor, often enough, since society and culture necessarily sanction only the best behaviour in these grave (!) circumstances, can there be even the minimal release of complaint. Is there a literature that talks of men who far prefer the company of nurses to that of their wives or children? Or of women who do not go to meet their unmakers with heads held less than nobly high, and goodness clasped to their breasts, or at least a full plan of their desired last rites? All of this may well be as it should be. Yet it will none the less shape the moving parts in the rack of individual grief that comes later.

*

ONE OF THE MANY reasons that rituals are important and necessary is that they abstract from individual experience and its inevitable failings and place it in a common stylized realm. All traditional cultures as well as contemporary secular ones engage in death rites. These put down markers in the vertiginous waves of mourning and the unchartable sea of experienced time. They take death and grief and place them in an external theatre where meaning, whether religious or secular, is conferred and shared, and social forms and norms re-established. In many cultures there is a funeral, a burial, and a further ceremony after a year, or thereabouts. For the Jews, this is often enough when the stone is set on the grave and the ghost placed firmly in the ground.

Palgi and Abramovitch have shown how in many non-literate societies death is met with two-fold mourning practices. During a first stage, the deceased is exposed to his mourners as a gruesome, decaying corpse. This is the social form that parallels the mourners' process of mental disintegration immediately following death. After a period of time, a second ritual sees the now bare bones of the dead moved to an ancestral site: this situates the dead as an object of worship and marks the reintegration of self and society in and for the mourners.

In the north-eastern corner of New Guinea, for example, the Ilahita people bury their dead in shallow or open graves in the dirt floors of domestic dwellings until the flesh has decomposed. As the body disintegrates and the reek diminishes, the accompanying fear of malicious ghosts, the torments of self-recrimination and guilt – what we could call the manifestation of ambivalence towards the dead – begin to subside as well. Once the bones are interred in the ancestral burial ground, the community as a whole celebrates the re-establishing of order.

In many cultures the bereaved spouse, sometimes the nearest relatives too, is isolated for a time, often enough a year, until the second ceremony takes place.

For those who might find such ritual practices a tad barbaric, or unseemly, I timidly suggest that our own prolonged ritual of probate, death duties and hungry attendant lawyers is only a very slightly cleaned-up state form of attack on the bereaved. He or she experiences the assault as an aggressive punishment by invisible forces, not a humane form of redistributing wealth, perhaps because a goodly portion of the redistribution goes into the hands of the legal guardians of the system who barely deserve it. But then, as the great anthropologist Jack Goody has noted, there ever seems to be a conflict between the mortality of the human body and the immortality of the body politic.

The anthropologist Hugh Brody, who spent many years living with the Inuit, a hunter-gatherer people in the far north of Canada, told me his local teacher there had an adopted son, a strong, energetic and jovial young man who was full of laughter. He would take Hugh out on long hunting trips with his dog team, and when they came back he would visit with his wife and children. They were friends.

After Hugh had been away for some months and returned to the village, he sought out his friend and asked him how he was. The man seemed transformed. He could barely speak. He was dull, unsmiling. He didn't want to do anything – this in a world where doing is all. Eventually, Brody learned that his friend's child had been killed in a fire. It was a terrible tragedy.

Time passed, and one day his friend, describing his parlous state, said to him, 'I lost my *isuma*.' '*Isuma*' is the Inuit word for mind. It's what develops through childhood. His friend had lost his mind with the loss of his child. Permission existed for this madness. His society accepted it.

The Inuit, like most hunter-gatherers, are low on ritual. When someone dies, the body is laid out in good clothes near where they died. Rocks are piled on the body, making a cairn. Often enough the inclement weather pulls the loose tumble of rocks apart and the body is devoured by animals. Only the bones are then visible. But the bones are recognized. Once, when Brody, on finding some bones in a field, asked whether an animal had been eaten there, he was told, 'No, that's my grandfather.'

Hugh's friend's mind came back, in part because his son had, too, in a reconfigured form. The family adopted a new baby and it was given his lost son's name. This is not only a naming rite, such as the Jews have in which the names of the recently dead may be attributed to new arrivals in the family. Neither is it quite the way in which we find the features, in our understanding caused by a genetic imprint, of the old in the newborn. In the Inuit case there is a belief that the name, let alone genes, is secondary to the fact that the dead have actually been incarnated in a new form. A baby may be called Grandma and grow up bearing the appellation of a dead grandmother, whose husband, while still alive, will also call her Grandma and treat the tiny babe or toddler with the respect due to the old.

Hugh's friend was no longer mad because his son had come back in a baby: his loss of mind and child were simultaneously restored.

14

THE FIRST TIME I WEPT – really wept, wept publicly, unstoppably – for John was at a book launch on 1 July, some eight months after he had died. You might be tempted to quip that, for writers, book launches have all the attributes of public ritual. But I think it was the specificity of this particular event that induced a sudden, utterly unexpected wave of tears and marked an important shift in my grief.

The crucible-like space was circular and dark and intimate. At first, I hadn't quite realized that we were standing on what was a small stage, with seats ranged above in the style of a Greek amphitheatre. The launch was for Hisham Matar's extraordinary memoir of his return to Libya to find the traces of his father, who had disappeared when Hisham was nineteen years old, some twenty-two years before, and had ended up in the vaults of Qaddafi's notorious Abu Salim prison. When exactly and how he had died is one of the mysteries the book tracks. It's a profound meditation on loss and lives intersected by politically wrought tragedy.

But the book was not why I wept. I had read it months before and, as with so much of my reading in those early months, I was able to gauge its brilliance but unable to feel its charge. My ability to feel was missing or massed in some inaccessible space, perhaps in the pre-verbal, since only the grandchildren and music seemed to provide access to it.

It was Hisham's spoken voice, its timbre, its slight hesitations, the immediacy of his tenderness, his felt humanity, that touched that chord. I'm not sure if he was talking about his father or his beloved wife, but suddenly the tears flooded. Neither the embarrassment, nor the lack of tissues or horrid sniffling would assuage them. I tried to hide, but moving while the speaking went on was impossible and the Monteverdi that followed only increased the flow.

I don't know whether the tears had suddenly erupted because I was also in the company of my old friend Albie Sachs, who was visiting from South Africa. Among much else, he was one of the judges who had written the country's new and exemplary constitution. He was also a man who had suffered so much more than I ever had, not only from imprisonment, solitary confinement, exile, but ultimately from a personalized bombing that had left him blind in one eye and without one arm. And yet he was somehow intact, without cynicism, imbued with at least the possibility of hope.

Hisham's father, Hisham himself, Albie: amid these three men who had endured so much, something in me must have felt I had permission to be moved.

15

I THINK IT WAS around that time that I started dreaming
again, or at least being woken abruptly in the middle of the
night by dreams I could just catch by the wisp of a tail. Nightmares, I guess, only partly recaptured, though what made them
so frightening was their all-too-quotidian matter. Dreams, in
some cultures, are thought to lie in that indeterminate realm
between the living and the dead. My interpretation is usually
far more prosaic. Nonetheless, if I couldn't fall asleep again,
and the wisps were still there, I might scrawl some notes.

I AM PART OF some kind of examining or prize-giving board.
A dozen or so judges are sitting around a large, squarish table
of shining mahogany. Several I recognize as writers, another
works for a charity, one for the civil service. The ceilings in the
room are very high, but so are the windows, ranged near the
top of one wall. We chit-chat. We are poised to begin when I
notice one of our judges is missing. 'Perhaps he's got lost,' I say.
'It's so easy to get lost with these endless corridors.' A woman
goes off to look for the missing judge. We are unable to begin.
I jerk awake in a panic.

WE ARE HAVING A PARTY – for our wonderful daughter. John has got in the wine and we've drawn up an expansive guest list across the generations. It isn't at home or, at least, not at the home I recognize. These rooms have odd boxlike shapes. We have been shopping. The glasses, the food, the flowers are all in place. The guests begin to arrive. I look around for John to help with things, but can't find him. I send one of the young ones to hunt for him upstairs. He's not there. He's not anywhere. I'm paralysed.

JOHN HAS LEFT EARLY for work and I'm still lying there. Suddenly there's a terrible noise from next door, banging and rising voices. I rush to the window. A dozen or more small people are pouring into the square garden. Not children but miniature people. At the centre of the garden there is a small ornate structure, like one of those Swiss cuckoo-clock houses, carved and ornamental, but the size of a gazebo. The raucous small people are crowding into it, dismantling parts and throwing them around in automaton glee. They're oddly dressed in breeches and they babble in a noisy incomprehensible language. They're frightening. I race for the phone. 'You've got to come home!' I shout. 'Quick! Something terrible has happened.'

I wake up in a sweat. My heart is racing. The house is silent.

I SUSPECT IT wouldn't take Freud to work out the principal substance of these dreams. My dead partner figures in them. He is present, even if I can't quite locate him. At least, at last, something is happening inside me. And the anger is now less abrasive and ever present.

By the time we gather at the graveside to mark the passage of a year, the rage has subsided or mutated into a form that has a largely political object and can give the aura of righteous heat. We place pebbles on the gravestone. My mother once told me they were there to make sure the unhappy spirits couldn't get out until the time was right. Superstition. But these shared rituals, with their readings and incantations, do soothe the troubled breast. And help us remember better.

When the *Prunus* flowers in the garden, some five months after that, I'm still dreaming but feel lighter in myself. When John was ill, a tree specialist knocked at the door and told us the tree had a cancer. I protested that it looked fine, had just suffered from dry weather. But, of course, we ended up paying him to apply whatever it was. We loved that tree. The year after John's death, it didn't look any better. The disease was wearing it down. It was distressing. The same specialist knocked at the door on three separate occasions and told me he would chop it down for a good price. I ended up by railing at him, shouting at him to leave me and my tree alone. He had done enough. He had killed it with his poison.

This year the tree wears a luxuriant robe of dark pink blossom and fresh leaf. The garden, which John treasured – digging, planting, pruning, keeping lists, while I dreamed colour and shape – is profligate in its bounty. Of such small restorations of the good does a kind of intermittent peace come. I have put his empty urn there, just in case he wants to have a look. I glance at it superstitiously and still feel some trepidation when I move a plant or two – an act he certainly would have chided.

16

THROUGH THOSE LONG months following John's death, I might not have been paying conscious attention to grieving, but I certainly had a new interest in death. Among the little I recall of the first half of the year, the death of David Bowie, a bare six weeks after my John, stands out. I listened to favourite tracks over and over again, and he came to me quite distinctly, not as his iconic stage presence but as the elegant and graciously courteous man I had met backstage in the eighties: the ICA, where I then worked, had put on a show called Intruders at the Palace. What I remember most clearly about him was the direct and unblinking way he met your eyes, even in a casual encounter.

Death had given me a new affinity with music. I had rarely had so much time or space to listen before. Now that I was alone, I did. Music filled the hollow spaces of the house. I listened to Bowie and more Bowie. I downloaded John's stored collection onto my own player. His music library, with its mass of old and new technologies, contained everything from competing versions of *The Marriage of Figaro* or Schubert's *Lieder* to Bob Dylan and Lily Allen. Though he played barely better than a beginner, he also had piano scores by the hundreds which he would sight-read to the family's chagrin. He was a collector there, too.

Playing John's music was perhaps another way of keeping him near and getting to know him better. I was constantly imagining where he had stood in relation to certain lyrics, what they had meant to him, why he had chosen one over another. Perhaps I was trying to appease the castigating bits of him (or, at least, I had attributed to him), which I had internalized, countering them with the more emollient sides of us both. And giving him a little distance. The music helped – it did indeed soothe the savage breast or, rather, the one that felt savaged.

Through those first eighteen months, I sometimes thought that I did my mourning for John – the sorrow that is also an anguished yearning for what is lost – in part by displacement. I mourned others. Their lives had a shape, a narrative. His was just too near, too much a part of myself for me to be able either to see him whole or to miss him, to long for him with the melancholy that ever has a tinge of romance. For months and months I was simply too ambivalent. But the grief, the grieving, that harsher, harder process, the one that cuts you up and tosses you about, was all for him. It came as no surprise that the linguistic origins of 'grieve' contain not only sorrow but all the associations with harm and oppression that have taken legal form in 'grievance'.

As the deaths of that year started to pile up, I began to feel there were more dead in my life than living.

The playwright Arnold Wesker had been one of my earliest friends in London and his home, with his wife, Dusty, one of the spaces that taught me the meaning of hospitality. When he died in April at the age of eighty-three, we had already for some time ceased to be very close. In the seventies, he had been a kind of godfather to my son, Josh, but when he moved out of London, in the way of things, life drew us apart. Yet every time we saw each other, it was as if no time had passed, and that witty, teasing, sparkling conversation began again. His death, the warm place he held in my heart, made me recognize that those strangers who had written or talked of my John as if they knew him intimately, possibly better than I did, though they rarely, if ever, saw him, did indeed hold something of him in their lives. Arnold felt no less close than he had so long ago: his voice was still there in the plays I reread and in my mind.

When my close friend and neighbour the novelist Sally Beauman died in July, only seventeen months after her husband, the actor Alan Howard, the loss felt like a body blow. In great sadness, but without tears, I wrote her obituary, and when I finished, the idea came to me that another year could well be all I needed to get through. That would go swiftly. I should start having dinner parties for the living and the dead. Celebrate their contiguity. Most of the dead were still friendlier than my John, but perhaps if I invited him along, if only to pour the wine and tell us a story about it, he would grow kinder.

By the time Leonard Cohen died, almost a year after John, I had built up an inner geography of death. People I had known well or encountered only once or twice inhabited discrete spaces within that landscape and opened avenues of association. Some reminded me that I had a past which was my own and not symbiotically shared. Oddly, the dead I had known less well or seen only irregularly, and more intensely because they lived at a distance, seemed more memorable, like those shared long-ago public events you can recall clearly while last week's dinner with a close friend vanishes into the ether. It's as if the mind finds repetition too tedious and relegates it to bodily familiarity. Or perhaps it was only that those distant ones already existed in a vaporous ether of the imagination, in some absence that had itself grown familiar. The fact that they could no longer be visited or reached on the phone arrived as a sporadic surprise.

I had known the great Leonard Cohen just a little when I was a stripling of a university student in Montréal and he was a dashing novelist and poet. He would come to one of our student haunts and we would all gather round, drawn by his wit and charm. Later, when he had grown famous, I interviewed him in London for a Montréal paper. When he died, on 7 November 2016, I dug out that interview from some yellowing bits of newsprint my mother had kept and were now stashed in a dusty, difficult-to-reach box. Embarrassing to read, with its evident trace of my attempt not to be utterly star-struck, it was yet material evidence that I had once had another life. I found myself weeping for Leonard Cohen, who had grown into such a graceful old age, for my mother, who had saved my clippings and loved me probably more than I loved myself. And for myself. I think I was crying for John, too, and resurrecting younger versions of him.

The day after Leonard Cohen died I finally managed to reach John Berger on the phone and express love and wishes, just two days late, for his ninetieth birthday. I had seen him in February not long after my John died. In fact, I had agreed to do some filming in Paris, because I so wanted to see him: during those early months, only work commitments, or sometimes the prodding of my children, spurred me into leaving home. It was as if wandering around the world, unanchored by a familiar to whom days and ways could be detailed morning and night, was too dangerous an undertaking. One might disappear ungracefully under a train, or accidentally accede to the tug of rushing water, or collapse crossing the street and tactlessly leave the young ones shocked and forced to pick up the pieces.

But I wanted, I needed, to see John B. I knew that every time I put it off, there might not be a next time. And I had always gone to see him at the various crossroads in my life. Not because he was a genius of a writer whose sentences and paragraphs prodded thought, and whose essays and fictions sparked a shift in one's ways of seeing and being. Not because he advised. Rarely that. But because his presence itself acted as a restorative power. Maybe it was the way he combined fierceness and stillness in the same breath.

With his two feet planted firmly on the ground, his forward thrusts of torso, his unruly shirts and hair, his clear blue always focused eyes, his cigarettes held in a stubby, expressive hand and glass of good plain red wine in the other, and, yes, his beauty, even greater as an old man, he was a force for life, for the very necessity of the human, for what was best in us.

I had known him for at least a decade longer than my John. We had history. He had met my parents, knew me from prior lives, and we had worked together, translated together, at various points shared manuscripts. He had stayed in the house for spans, often with his final partner, Nella. In the old days, we used to walk our boys (his youngest and my eldest) together to Waterlow Park and Highgate Cemetery, where various toddler antics took place close to the oversized material solidity of Karl Marx's tomb. John B's laugh, which started hesitant, then boomed so loud it benefited from open space, could be heard reverberating across the graves. I think he must have made the dead happy.

That cold, wet and dismal February afternoon, I made the RER trip from central Paris to the modest house in Antony where he lived with Nella. It was a house that was as Russian, or certainly Eastern European, as it was French. White cloths, sometimes embroidered, covered the tables. There was a piano, wearing photographs. There were always flowers and the smell of home cooking. If I can still unearth such dim memories, it had something about it of the house my parents lived in when I was very small.

John was lying on the day-bed in the little conservatory where the light from the outdoors was at its brightest grey. At first, I wasn't sure he recognized me. He had been dozing or in a trance. He had long been friendly with his dead. It had seemed to me that his wife Beverly's death some four years earlier had brought him very close to the edge. He was almost lost to us then. But he had come back, at least for a short while, I now told myself with a shiver.

But then he was up and swept aside all such grim thoughts. He said my name with the particular inflection of surprise, pleasure and assertion that was his alone and embraced me, all the while murmuring, 'There, there.'

JOHN'S 'THERE, THERE,' is not only an expression of consolation. It's a way of holding of itself. Like his presence, it holds you. And it holds you 'there', firmly placed as an inhabitant of this earth, let alone this special corner of it. It's a habitation all of its own.

I've often wondered whether it was John's presence (sensed even through the eyes of a camera – remember his direct, almost visceral, address to it and to us in *Ways of Seeing*) that made his evocations of place in his writing so habitable. Or was it his ability to conjure place up that gave him such spatial presence? There's no answer. His writing on art *places* you, places you right in front of the canvas, perhaps even in the strokes the artist makes. I remember once, long ago, going to an exhibition with him, standing in front of a Cézanne and saying to John that Cézanne had never really spoken to me – he felt too formal.

John made that funny noise in his throat, part impatience, part hesitation, part 'aah', and stepped in front of the canvas. With a few deft gestures and murmurs of 'See: there, there, there,' Cézanne suddenly made sense – his laying on of colour, like a path through space, his bodies dense places of light and shade.

John knew about place, the inhabiting of it and the leaving of it. His unique inflection of Marxism apart – a kind of sense of justice that stretched to all the disinherited of the earth – I think he wrote about migrants and immigrants before so many others because he had a deep, bodily understanding of displacement, what it meant to be forced to leave one's place and somehow create another. Leavings, trains, cars, motorbikes, elusive destinations, lines through space, like promises, sometimes broken, are frequent in his writing. He used to send or give me drawings now and again – a pomegranate, a hand outstretched, the Polish Rider astride his horse going, just going. And once, very early on, a painting of men in a boat, sailing nowhere, but hard at it.

When I said to him once – we were at my place – that I wished I could draw or, above all, paint, he planted his feet firmly on the floor as if it were ground and pointed at or made shapes of the various spaces around him and said, 'But this is your canvas, this . . . there . . . there . . . this house, this home.' I didn't respond, as I might have done, with a sense of little woman being put down, worn down, like Louise Bourgeois' famous *Femme Maison* (*House Woman*, or *Housewife*), with a house for a head. That wasn't the spirit of his remark. Instead I felt enlarged and thought, yes, it was true, I treated my home as a canvas that was always evolving, a space for us all, a habitation.

Habitations are made of habits, which is what brush strokes, applied over and over again, are, too. So are words, or I think they were for John, a master of them, presences requiring placement, arrangement, over and over again. His letters were always full of crossings out, of arrows.

Then there are the habits of everyday life, out of which we make our relationships and our homes.

I remember John arriving at ours bearing a tray of snails in garlic sauce from Paris, a special treat for dinner that evening.

The careful way he lifted them from their box and placed them one by one precisely on a large plate felt like an act of love. His presence was in each simple, habitual movement.

John was as present in his listening as in his acts. One time, many years ago – I was still young and had gone to see him in the mountains of the Haute Savoie – we were driving in his old Deux Chevaux through the curving mountain roads when I asked him where his ideas came from. He chuckled. 'I don't have ideas. They don't come,' he said to me. I had been complaining that I didn't know what to write next. 'I listen. Yes!' He countered the scepticism with which I usually greeted his more oracular comments. 'I simply listen.'

As the days in the tiny hamlet unfolded, I realized this was true. The little house, where cows had once sheltered from the cold on the upstairs floor and warmed its downstairs residents, was more of a social hub than many a café. Neighbours never stopped dropping in, having a coffee or a *gnôle* and talking, talking, talking. John, meanwhile, listened, gave everyone additional presence through his own, so that they went away feeling enlarged, placed.

Later, when I knew more about such things, I thought maybe he had learned something about listening from the great child analyst, D. W. Winnicott, whose upstairs lodger he was, sometime in the fifties. But John's listening, the intensity of his presence and the sharing of it with another, was just part of his thereness, in which you were included.

I am no philosopher, I have no mystic inclinations, but when I left John, that afternoon in February 2016, I felt better, as if bits of me might have been rearranged in a less abased place. And intensely sad. I had no idea that the next day John would have to return home ill after an abortive trip to the Berlin Biennale.

When I learned of this illness – I don't know why, but I was still enmeshed in the superstitious paranoia that for so many makes up part of the early grieving process – I thought of Primo Levi. I had met the great man once, and he had about him a stillness that was not unlike John's, but in him it was coupled with a cool diffidence and a different kind of gentleness. It was soon after my daughter was born. I was back at work at the ICA, a little sporadically, and on that day she had come with me, as had my mother to walk her in the park while the conversation with Primo Levi went on. Over lunch, he held the baby with a tenderness I thought remarkable in a man I had only just met and one who had been through so much. She evidently liked him too, holding his gaze and refraining from any squalls. He spoke to my mother at great length as well, sharing histories, in the way of those of that generation, who had been through the worst.

Soon enough after his return to Italy, Primo Levi died, some say having committed suicide. I kept seeing him with my baby daughter in his arms and couldn't believe it.

Though John Berger and I spoke again on several occasions, that February in Paris was the last time I saw him. When he died, almost a year later, I wept. The sadness, free of panic, guilt, abasement, deranged thoughts, was for my John, too. I was feeling again. Feeling something that wasn't rage and wasn't plagued by pernicious racing thoughts.

At last.

LOSING

I'm not lost for I know where I am. But, however, where I am may be lost.

A. A. MILNE, Winnie-the-Pooh

1

IN OLD ENGLISH, *los* means destruction. We lose a near one and suffer a loss. This may make you 'lose it' – lose your temper, your grip on reason, your self-control or, indeed, your very self.

I wonder whether I was lucky in that my private loss occurred at a time when Britain itself seemed to be losing it, a condition we shared with our American cousins. My grieving was in tune with the times. It may also be that the times exacerbated my own condition or, alternatively, hid it. Everyone was angry. We were all raging losers.

In the lead-up to and after the referendum on staying in or leaving the EU, and in the period before and after the American election, rage seemed to spread by osmosis. The body politic erupted with it, civic space grew uncivil with it, and the virtual (often unsocial) sphere waxed more choleric and bilious than an old alcoholic waking from a really bad night.

I am walking along towards the exit of a very busy London Underground platform. Walking is an exaggeration. A slow shuffle is what I'm doing. We are all being propelled by the people behind us. Inevitably from time to time we abut each other.

Halfway to the exit the man just in front rounds on me. He is a good foot, or more, taller than I am and twice as broad.

'You fucking cunt,' he shouts. 'Stop pushing.'

Needless to say, any protest, or explanation that the person behind and the next and the next and everyone in the long queue is pressing against each other, is in vain. Reason is not at home here.

I am shaken. And in turn I am angry, though my anger is as nothing to the rage of the man in front, who continues to curse and threaten as the crush creeps forward. The stick of his size and voice speaks loudly, as does the heat of his bile. He feels dangerous. My attempt at protest dies in my throat.

By the time we near the escalators, I have managed to put a few bodies' distance between us. Now shame and helpless frustration join my anger. Why didn't I scream? Why couldn't I punch him? My heart is racing frantically. Already I've begun to blame myself. Was it my fault? Had I done something wrong? I should have punched him, not myself.

A young woman behind me asks, 'Are you okay?' She has evidently witnessed the scene. She's tall with flaming red hair and dressed all in dramatic black. 'Pay no attention,' she soothes. 'He's crazy. They're all crazy, these days.'

2

THESE DAYS ARE the days of Brexit and Donald Trump. Populist leaders and movements are on the rise across parts of Europe and also in Russia and India. What they have in common is that they engage in the politics of emotion and dress up the old tools of propaganda in shiny new hyperbolic forms. What they're really good at is creating enemies and stoking hatred.

These days are also, and have long been, the days of sexual predation. This has reached a peak that women no longer want to tolerate. Men have long raged at women in all the guises we take on through life, and thus re-enacted the childhood diminishment they may have felt at the hands of Mum or Dad, who was angry with Mum. Like the playground bully, such men act big and horrible and are dangerous when perhaps they feel at their smallest. Women are now raging back, angry with the men who have diminished them, but also angry with themselves for having put up with what they now assess they didn't want.

I try to make sense of this new world of unleashed hatreds, my own, too, of a vituperative willingness to engage in bad behaviour, of a two fingers up to a liberal consensus which had at least *declared* it good that people of all colours, genders and kinds be treated equally and with respect. With trust, too, the glue that allows society to function.

During the referendum campaign, with its appeal on the leave side to emotions unhindered by fact, anger was fuelled. The EU, with its free movement of labour, its invisible bankers, its experts, its speakers of bureaucratic reason, its rules and rights, was targeted as the cause of all of Britain's ills. Wresting control from it seemed to provide an excuse for being out of control at home. It was not so much a question of 'taking control' back to Parliament as of unleashing self-control in the name of 'righteous' rage.

When talk of control is in the offing, you can bet your vocal cords someone is out of control.

Populists and revolutionaries have long known that resentment, or its more virtuous political namesake from the nineteenth century, *ressentiment*, can be the crucible for explosive acts. Humiliations, grievances, envies, a host of slights and individual failures amass and find succour, even the balm of holiness, under a collective banner, usually waved about by a man, more rarely a woman, with the gift of the gab. On occasion, the banner has justice on its side.

Ever since the attack on Manhattan's Twin Towers, when the *ressentiment* of the Middle East found expression on the relatively untouched soil of America, it was clear that explosive rage against the rampant power, the riches and relatively secular values of the West and its version of globalism, was to be the toxic flavour of the new century. The old Cold War divisions that had siphoned differences into the capacious and a-religious headings of Communism versus capitalism, largely giving each a geographic location, had crumbled with the Berlin Wall in 1989.

I was around through all that. And well before. I watched the political shifts, sniffed the changing densities of atmosphere. You may not remember all the dailiness of history when you've lived through it, but if your senses are alert to streets and salons, as well as the news and taking your children through their own changes and schooling and metamorphoses of taste, you may willy-nilly end up knowing a few things.

What I know is that, fed by feelings of powerlessness, humiliation and a potent addition of envy – the emotion that begrudges the good fortune and gifts of others – existential resentment doesn't need geography to flourish. East versus West, socialism versus capitalism, a longing for an ordered authoritarian, religious state rather than a liberal, permissive 'modern' one, these old antagonists are now neighbours on each other's terrain, physically in the same land, inhabiting the same cities. If not, they're certainly virtual neighbours. As such, they seep into one another, breeding phantasms in the mind.

I need never have encountered an Islamist or a Christian pro-life fundamentalist of the kind that rule the world of Margaret Atwood's *The Handmaid's Tale*. Yet they live inside me, their images as clear and terror-inducing as if they lived next door – in fact more so, since the global reach of the Web and social, as well as news, media bring them inside my room and, with their reduced lineaments all shaped in the contours of fear, inside my imagination. Here they strut, woman-haters to a man, purveyors of purity, who would inevitably prefer to deny that they have been born of woman and prior acts of fornication.

The misogynistic elites of purity have long elicited my anger. In turn I and my kind are targets for their rage. But other elites have also long been and are now again central targets in the populist landscape of resentment.

Aristocrats, landowners, the rich, bankers, capitalists – with their hold on power and privilege – have perennially infuriated those who became the traditional militants of the left. Today when the old left/right designations that stem from French Revolutionary times have been emptied of a quantum of their meaning, they serve as targets of anger for the right as well – as they once did in Weimar Germany.

In Britain and the US, where experts are cyclically honoured and despised, a varied elite can often enough be compounded into a single anger-inducing entity. Scientists, academics and technocrats, who are rarely the highest earners, are cast into the same sinkable boat as the very rich – though the last in the US are also admired, whatever the dubious means by which they may have acquired their wealth.

Way back in the turbulent decades of the belle époque (1871–1914), when a modern democracy was taking shape in France, the sociologist Gustave Le Bon worried over the psychology of the ever-labile, ever-suggestible 'crowd'. The times bore a resemblance to our own. Unemployment, great disparities between rich and poor, impoverishment of the countryside, large-scale immigration from the East and from country to city, a Catholic backlash against liberal values and women's agitation for equality, fear about changing gender roles, anarchist bombs inducing terror, a powerful press more interested in sensation than sense: all contributed to Le Bon's anxieties about populist uprising. Among much else, the tabloids, with their mass readership, abetted anti-Semitism and rage over the Dreyfus affair, itself created by alternative 'facts' which singled out a Jewish officer for an act of treason committed by another.

'Affirmation pure and simple, kept free of all reasoning and all proof,' Le Bon wrote in *The Crowd* (1895), 'is one of the surest means of making an idea enter the mind of crowds. The more concise an affirmation is, the more destitute of every appearance of proof and demonstration, the more weight it carries.' Any campaign-managing professional repeats that mantra daily. 'America First', 'Make America Great Again', 'Stable and Strong', 'Take Back Control', 'Brexit means Brexit'.

In an attention economy, where everyone suffers in one degree or another from its deficit, the most important asset is to be able to monopolize attention. Trump has done this expertly. His strutting, and tweeting, his celebrity antics have made his brand the most famous one in the world, apparently by a factor of nine. Hypnotizing the population was what Le Bon feared and warned against most, since it would devastate the new democracy that the Third Republic was. What hypnotism purportedly does is focus the attention of the subject on a single object, a single other, submitting to his greater power. Trump has hypnotized the world, expertly ensuring that he acts as its central focus. Anger is one of his tools.

Since the populist banner trumpets simple solutions for complex problems, a scapegoat is often named as the cause of all of society's ills. The scapegoat invariably wears a label of otherness – skin colour, religion, national origin, migrant, even simply European will do. So will gender. Our liberal democracies grow increasingly illiberal.

3

I HAVE ALWAYS BEEN nervous of crowds. And of simplified certainties.

I don't know if it's because, as a small child, I was placed in a situation where I was jostled and tugged and propelled among knees, and people were shouting. Or because I'm small and can't see over people's heads to check what's happening at the front of the massed bodies. Or because you never know when the crowd might turn into a mass that hurtles you in a direction you don't want to take, particularly if the police are present. Or because, in the swarm, any semblance of individual limits or reservations disappears. Neither have I ever found an ego-ideal, as Freud might say, a leader out there in the world in whom I want to subsume my identity with a group of unnamed others.

Maybe I'm just subject to some more atavistic anxiety about the crowd, which is linked to family lore conveyed to me before I reached any age of reason.

Of course I've been on demos and marches. In my teenage years, as a reporter for the university newspaper, I marched with the Separatists in Montréal. Later there were anti-Vietnam war rallies in London, protests against the poll tax, women's marches . . . But the vocal solidarity, the 'high' of group protest, has never altogether put an underlying unease to rest. I don't like places where people are crammed together and in the sway of, or cheering, distant politicians, particularly when that political performance is calculated to deliver a visceral punch.

A rumble of fear takes me over if anger is roused: the crowd may turn into a pack, whether hunting others or myself. Politics that work on the emotions fill me with instant distrust. Even when I may agree with their content, I can sniff violence building in the air.

Hitler's orchestrated massed rallies and parades, with their medieval emblems and choreographed salutes, waving banners and rasping, frenzied, hypnotic Führer's voice. Mussolini's grandstanding from operatic balconies. Lenin's revolutionary heat and sloganeering. Castro's unending, hypnotizing oratory. Boris Johnson's stutters, preceding a flurry of hair and metaphorized verbiage. Trump's lacquered swirl of gold, like a pop star's crown, his gestures of voice and hand learned from bossing people around reality TV, his use of hyperbole and the emphatic demotic 'one big thing' . . . In an ideal world, I'd want to stop them all, not least from infiltrating my mind and taking it over, which is precisely what they're geared to do.

I was hardly alone in these last years to discover that a toxic political climate had invaded my imagination, my dreams, and my own sense of reality. London therapists in the wake of Brexit found that politics had moved into the consulting room and were creating or increasing individual anxiety. The condition, dubbed 'Brexit anxiety', leaves people feeling out of control, unable to influence the direction of their lives or relationships, or recognize the city they used to call home. A 'learned helplessness', one of the bases of depression, is the result. School bullying, racism, anti-Semitism, and Islamophobia are part of the picture. These put parents, particularly from mixed ethnicity families, into a precarious position: people don't know how to cope.

As my grieving collided with national anger and a sense of helplessness, I found my own state reflected in and augmented by the warring voices on screen and radio. People were suddenly talking over each other in rarely witnessed and incomprehensible fury. Presidential supporters, hair flying, eyes flashing, railed against opponents. Brexiteers huffed and puffed while Remainers choked and spluttered. Moderators became immoderate, an indistinguishable screech in the general fray. Everyone seemed to have the permission of the broadcasters to rage.

Words had lost their sense. Only the heat of emotion, the rowing frenzy mattered. The chattering monkeys of the distraught inner state had taken over the public air waves. And they were self-righteous with it. They might not have looked like the raging primates with bared teeth and wild stare ethologist Desmond Morris describes in *The Naked Ape*, but they were certainly making loud sounds and inflating themselves to look larger and fiercer, in tandem with our animal kin.

4

WE ARE IN OUR FOURTH – or is it fifth? – house in Montréal, the ultimate lap of a journey that brought my parents and their two children, of whom I was the younger, from post-war Poland, via France to Canada. We are by this time – it is five or six years since our arrival as immigrants – modestly comfortable, at least financially, and the house is a new one purchased off an architect's plan for a housing development. There are as yet no trees. The area is flat, bounded only by train tracks and a golf club that doesn't admit Jews. As history keeps showing us – though in our wish to think better of our human kin and ourselves, we don't like to admit it – being victim to atrocity doesn't necessarily seem to make people more loved. At least not until they've washed themselves of the first signs of damage and behave more like everyone else, or maybe just grow richer – though not too rich.

My mother stands in front of the bathroom mirror. She is putting on foundation cream, eye shadow, lipstick. She makes those strange faces people do when applying cosmetics. A lift and stretch of bright blue eye, a trance-like stare, a pout, a pressing of red lip on lip, a movie-star smile.

My father is waiting for her to drive to work. They work together. She is always too slow. He is always in a hurry.

I'm standing by the bathroom door waiting for my turn to go in and watching. My parents usually drop me off at school on their way to work.

Suddenly my father erupts, cursing in every language he has to hand, telling her to get a move on. Each word is a whiplash of foaming hatred. His face is contorted. In my memory he looks like one of those Messerschmidt heads, gaping mouth a black hole, teeth bared, eyes screwed up tight, a frightening mad person.

Then the door bangs and he is out of the house.

Meanwhile my mother stiffens and slowly concentrates on her cheeks. She carries on applying a little rouge, hardly missing a beat. Finished, she offers a tuneless whistle, picks up her handbag and a coat or tailored jacket, all the while repeating that my father is in a hurry.

Please remember, my parents love each other, are deeply attached day and night, night and day.

The whole time we drive along the suburban streets, stop at traffic lights, climb up a hill, my mother makes random chitchat. My father is grim and silent, revving noisily as we leave lights and braking hard as we reach them. Getting out at the school gates some ten minutes away is a relief.

Thanks to this daily ritual, even if I can't speak more than a few short sentences of Polish, I can still swear like a trooper.

I also know the face of rage.

5

I FIRST READ James Joyce's *Dubliners* when I was sixteen, early in my university life. Despite rereadings, the only story apart from 'The Dead' that has stayed in my mind, as a live rather than shadowy presence, is 'Counterparts'.

It's a singularly chilling tale, at least for me, and I have occasionally wondered why. Joyce explores the trapped impotence of Farrington, a lowly copyist, a maker of counterparts or duplicates in a legal firm in which the menacing boss – a certain Mr Alleyne from the North of Ireland, coded Protestant, a small man with a big voice and a head 'so pink and hairless it seemed like a large egg reposing on the papers' – has it in for his employee.

But if the worker is a tool of the system, his alienation in this story is in large part also his own doing. Farrington, who is 'tall and of great bulk', with a wine-coloured, hanging face, and heavy, dirty, bulging eyes, is a shirker, a liar and a drinker. He sneaks off to the pub at every opportunity.

Joyce charts the humiliations of his day. Chastised for not having a contract ready, Farrington shows off by behaving impertinently in front of Mr Alleyne's lady friend: he replies to his boss's question 'Do you think me an utter fool?' that this is hardly a fair question to put to him. It's a clever reply with which he'll regale his pub friends. First, however, he is forced to apologize or lose his job.

Feeling savage, thirsty and revengeful, Farrington has to pawn his watch in order to spend an evening in a pub crawl. He stands rounds for his cronies and regales them over and over with his cheeky repartee until it loses its charge. The English-woman he fancies won't return his gaze. The stripling of an Englishman he resents having bought drinks for boasts of his muscles, and Farrington is urged to uphold national honour in an arm-wrestling competition. He loses.

He grows increasingly sullen and irate, mulling over the day's humiliations. By the time he reaches home to call for his wife, 'who bullied him when he was sober and was bullied by him when he was drunk', only to find her out, he turns his drunken rage on his small son, striking him vigorously with his walking stick. In vain, the boy pleads, 'Don't beat me, Pa. I'll say a Hail Mary for you.'

This repetition, this counterparting of bilious rage as it passes from the small, shouting boss to the lumbering, increas-ingly animal-like, enraged Farrington, and then in an explosion of physical violence to the small, frail innocent is an intimate portrait of the psychology of bullying. Only divine intercession can help the child.

It's a long shot. A howl of desperation.

6

In his essay 'On Anger', the great Montaigne writes:

> No passion disturbs the soundness of our
> judgement as anger does. No one would hesitate to
> punish with death a judge who was led to condemn
> his man as a criminal out of anger: then why is it any
> more permissible for fathers and schoolmasters to
> punish and flog children in anger? That is no longer
> correction, it is vengeance.

Rage terrifies me. I know that. It's beyond reason. Beyond reasoning with. Beyond language.

That my response is instinctual, an animal reaction to threat, doesn't seem to explain enough. Neither my friends in life nor in books seem quite so sensitively alert to it.

I was not an abused child, neither in the sexual sense that the word 'abuse' took on in the 1990s nor in the prior sense of a 'beaten' child. But, like everyone else, I have been a child. Tiny, powerless, vulnerable, without much voice, apart from that inchoate scream one can never altogether imagine coming out of one's own chest and mouth as time rolls one into adulthood.

True, in the way of the times, my father smacked me now and again. He once even took a belt to me. I think, judging by the boxlike room of my memory, I must have been around eight years old. We were living at our third Canadian address, an apartment in the Snowdon area of Montréal, just below the penitential mount of St Joseph's Oratory where the Catholic pilgrims climbed the steep external stairs on their knees, seeking absolution from their sins. Perversely, because of the romance of it, come adolescence we all gathered there on Christmas Eve for midnight mass whether we were Christian or not.

My father's outburst was frightening. So frightening I can still clearly remember his gesture of exasperation as he pulled the belt from his trousers and ordered me to lie down. Did he feel angrier with himself and my mother, who had driven him to the punishment, than with me? Or is that my own later exoneration of him? The thwack came in any case, once, twice, perhaps a third time. I howled and howled for what felt like hours in disproportionate terror. I can still taste the salt of the tears, see the puddle of discolouring moisture on the white pillowcase. But I can no longer recall the wrong I was meant to have committed.

I do remember that I felt outraged at the injustice of it. After all, I would stand at the dark window of the apartment, writing in the mist my breathing made, and longing for my parents' return with an anguish that still hovers close when I need now to wait for a near one. I loved my father and I thought he loved me: they always said I was the apple of his eye.

So why was I being punished so aggressively after all that waiting?

Perhaps I was just outraged that my mother – or was it my brother? – had carried tales, and that my father would believe them to the point of administering violence. But it could well have been otherwise.

Under the cultural settlements for child-rearing in the distant fifties, this event did not mark a cruel and unusual punishment. Schools were still regularly administering thrashings. Teachers themselves walked round with rulers that were regularly whacked down on desks or on fingers and hands at the slightest provocation. Heads were even more brutal in their ministrations. Looking after children involved physical discipline and corporal punishment. They were animals after all. To be shaped into law-abiding humans. That was just the way it was. Patriarchal authority was a given society agreed upon.

After one of her two young heroines, Lila, has been thrown from a window by her loving father, Elena Ferrante describes in an unsentimental way the violence that was a matter of course in the impoverished outskirts of Naples in the post-war period: 'Men returned home [from the Bar Solara] embittered by losses, by alcohol, by debts, by deadlines, by beatings, and at the first inopportune word they beat their families, a chain of wrongs that generated wrongs.' Echoes of Joyce's 'Counterparts' a half-century later.

In my primary-school days largely in Montréal, I received the ruler's angry rap – several times on each palm – on only one occasion, before being ordered to stand in the corner, a humiliated little girl who refused to cry. I had corrected the teacher's French. She was an English speaker. I knew I spoke better than she, it being my almost native language, even if several others rolled around the familial home. I couldn't work out whether I was being punished for being right or for having dared to correct the teacher. Both seemed equal sins. But I wouldn't cry, not in front of everyone. Even though I was a good sobber into pillows.

But these two rather minor experiences of adult brutality are hardly enough to explain my terror at the volcanic rage of others – so emphatic that I have run out on any man who threatened. John, my partner of over thirty years, rarely raised his voice and only once erupted. And he was always on time. I suspect the quiet, the even temper, was part of the attraction.

When someone is very angry, I simply leave. I leave the room or the house or perhaps myself as well.

Is this why in the various books I've written exploring madness or extremes of passion, I have never really focused on anger, that altogether ordinary, quotidian emotion – but one that can wreak total havoc?

7

WHERE I HAVE confronted anger's workings in my books, it was always in an attempt to understand the dark side of love – the jealous rage of an Othello, the fury of a woman betrayed, like Marie Bière who helped launch a fashion in revenge against philandering men in 1880s France. She used a revolver. Others employed vitriol, which left its vitriolic trace in the vocabulary.

But the anger spectrum is far broader and more varied than that. It could be said to entail everything from a toddler's tantrum to the critic's curled lip of stubborn dismissiveness. The growl of everyday exasperation at unopenable jars, telephone queues, hiccups in on-line form filling – in other words mute, buried, or mildly expressed irritation at contemporary days and ways – marks another point on the anger chart. So does throwing crockery at spouses or hurling abuse at people on the tube or at home, and unswayable bitterness or negativity.

Some of the feelings within the anger constellation can culminate in the explosions of fury that lead to murder or indeed self-murder. As can protracted resentment, especially when shored up and inflamed by a group or ideology that shouts simple solutions to the inchoate ills experienced by the individual.

Fury was long a word associated with deranged passion. Rage is why the mad were kept locked in chains. Jean-Étienne Esquirol – from 1811 until his death in 1840, a pioneer of the humane treatment of the mentally ill and of the systematic description of mental disturbance – thought of mental illness as an excess of the ordinary passions that 'spring from the first wants of man – love, anger, jealousy'.

In his treatise on insanity, *Mental Maladies*, he noted: 'All the passions have their seasons of fury. In their excesses, there is nothing that they do not sacrifice; and man while a prey to passion, spares not his own life.'

One of the inmates he describes is an angry man who 'breaks, rends, and destroys, whatever comes within his reach. He cries aloud, threatens and strikes, alleging always a motive *to justify* the frightful disorder of his actions.' Anger can be persistent; rage is intermittent – an outburst, an expression of other difficulties rather than a core condition.

The latest edition, the fifth, of the American bible of mental medicine, *Diagnostic and Statistical Manual of Mental Disorders* (*DSM*) lists an Intermittent Explosive Disorder (IED), characterized by outbursts of anger and unpremeditated violence that are disproportionate to events or triggering phenomena. Occurring in the category of 'Disruptive, Impulse-Control and Conduct Disorders', IED is often found alongside substance abuse and bipolar conditions, as well as post-traumatic stress disorder (PTSD). As a change from the earlier, fourth, *DSM*, which limited the disorder to rage that abutted on *physical* violence, IED can now also include episodes of verbal aggression, which are non-injurious physically – 'tirades, verbal arguments/fights, or assault without damage'. For a diagnosis, these need to occur on average twice weekly for three months.

Judging by the proliferation of anger-management sites and counselling services the Web offers, our world contains many explosive people. A proportion of them have suffered workplace or marital breakdown. Others are adolescents. Boys and young men in particular are prone to explosive, sometimes dangerous behaviour: armies down the ages have known how to make use of this and sometimes named it heroism. Shakespeare's over-bold Sir Harry 'Hotspur' says it all in his nickname, appropriately adopted by a London football club. Hotspur's wife teasingly calls him 'a mad-headed ape'.

The testosterone surges that affect adolescent men are said to flatten fear and disinhibit. As neurologists indicate, the prefrontal cortex is not yet fully articulated in teenagers. This leaves judgement and self-regulation at the mercy of fierce impulses. I always visualize my then fifteen-year-old son, new to skiing, hurling himself down a precarious black run, arms akimbo and shouting joyfully. Or, with equal alacrity, snapping at his parents in short-lived rage.

Talking boys down from (recurrent) explosions requires what psychologists call 'engaging several modalities'. It's not that boys don't hear parents as well as most girls do, it's just that, psychologists note, they often don't interpret or take in what is said, unless you engage their eyes and touch them simultaneously.

Courses of psychotropic medications have limited success with IED. In many cases it would be far better for those diagnosed with it to be weaned off drink and drugs, both known for their disinhibiting effects. Cognitive behavioural therapies have better results, as do any therapies that target so-called impulse control by raising the level at which anger occurs in response to real or imagined provocation.

But anger, volcanically displayed, controlled or repressed, seems to be fundamental to humans as well as many animals. Behaviourists see it as part of the fight or flight apparatus we all have when we sense threat. Their key originating source for linking humans and animals here is Charles Darwin. In describing the underlying characteristics of rage, Darwin – who sees emotions as inextricably allied to their expression – points to the physical features that mark and indeed *are* the state in its primary characteristics: the acceleration or disturbance of the heart, a reddening or 'deadly pallor' of the face – the latter indicating the flow of blood has been impeded so that the person, already suffering from heart disease, may drop down dead. There is laboured respiration, a quivering of dilated nostrils, a glistening of eyes 'with fire', all of which take place involuntarily. The posture – raising of the arms, clenched fists and teeth – indicates the need to strike out, to fight. Toddlers, like young apes, roll on the ground in rage, kicking, scratching and biting, in what we call a tantrum.

Darwin also describes as emotions related to anger, indignation, sneering and defiance, all of which find parallels in the animal world.

The anger spectrum seems always to be with us. At times its collective expressions, the violence it tumbles into, are particularly marked.

After the senseless manifestation of the international explosive disorder that was the First World War, Freud – who never directly linked his new thinking with that destructive event – posited a death principle or drive, the propulsive force of aggression, a death wish to sit alongside the pleasure principle. Human motivation could not be explained by a desire for pleasure or life alone.

8

It's a dank, drizzly day and I'm driving along Spaniard's Road, with its ranked mass of generous trees at the top end of Hampstead Heath. Potholes pit the road, despite the swanky postcode and capacious houses. These and the increasing density of traffic may be what encouraged the council to put a 20 m.p.h. speed limit on the road.

I'm pottering along in my minuscule black car, thinking about Hitchcock's *Dial M for Murder*. I watched it again recently and found myself fascinated that, even to a greater degree than in *Rear Window*, the action rarely leaves the single stagey room. Behind its thick, dark curtains, the murderer – who is an old school acquaintance of the scheming husband – has been ordered to hide. Those curtains resemble the ones in my front room where I found the window forced open by a wannabe burglar just after my John died.

It's perhaps this event that has now given the film an extra spooky resonance for me. Or maybe it's Grace Kelly's chilling performance as a wife in the claustrophobic Hitchcock-Gothic of her imprisoning environment: the way she moves from being a confident, coolly sensual woman to a broken victim, condemned to death for a violent crime enacted in self-defence, the unintended result of her husband's plot to have her murdered so that he can be left free and enriched.

The balletic and beautiful Grace in her clarity of feature reminds me of the photographs of my mother in her pre-war and wartime youth. Hitchcock is the master of the handbag. The one he has given Grace to contain the tell-tale key is a double of one of my mother's. The bag's movement in the film – from Grace, to her husband, to the police inspector – carries all the menace of the mounting action. The psychological threat is in large part achieved by what goes under the name of 'gaslighting' – that mixture of lies, denial, misdirection, and often charming manipulation of effects, which cumulatively act to undermine the target's trust in her perceptions and sense of reality. In the film, *Gaslight*, from which the term comes, a predatory husband drives his wife to breakdown. In *Dial M for Murder*, Grace Kelly, by the eve of her execution, is a sleepwalker, a listless, unhearing puppet with no inhabiting will of her own, prey only to the male forces around her. Her key no longer fits in her own lock.

I wake from the trance of these rambling, desolate thoughts to the urgent sound of a horn behind me. In my rear-view mirror, I see a large, sleek car almost on my bumper, urging me into greater speed. I check and see that I'm already above the limit and doing 25 m.p.h. I press on the accelerator, but there's a slight bend in the road, where a friend's son once lost control of his car, and I'm reluctant to go much faster.

The hooting grows insistent. Abruptly the menacing car darts out to overtake me and cuts me off as it comes back into the lane, almost clipping the front of my car in the process, and narrowly missing an oncoming vehicle.

What an arsehole. Anger erupts and I, too, press my hand on my horn in cacophony with that of the oncoming vehicle's. 'Bastard,' I swear. A veritable idiot. My rage rises as I remember that ever since I bought this tiny black car I've been bullied on the roads. Surely it's the car these big bastards hate and not me, or can they see that I'm a diminished woman, past her prime, who is only good for bullying? Or is it that my driving has got that much worse?

I hear my daughter's voice repeating how I always go around blaming myself without first assessing the actions of others – she doesn't need to add, 'like a typical woman of your generation'.

I remind myself that nobody ever hooted at my previous car, luminous, puke green, acquired cheap. It looked like but wasn't a sports model. I also remind myself that everyone is short-tempered and explosive in these days of irate populist politics. All my friends complain of road rage. The country is incandescent.

By this time I've reached the traffic lights and, lo and behold, the culprit is stuck behind them. Just like me. Ha! I'm still raging and hoot and flash him a couple of times. A tubby beshirted figure of middle height with a bullet head emerges from the car and hulks towards me with a raised fist. He hits it against my closed window and shouts, 'Stupid bitch.' The car behind me starts to hoot, so does another further down the row. I raise two fingers at my assailant, who, having given my window a second thump, marches back to his car.

When I get to my destination, I'm so depleted I'm ready to go and join John in his grave. At least, there are no cars there.

9

FROM THE VANTAGE-POINT of the present, it sometimes seems that a rather large proportion of my remembered childhood unfurled in cars. Distances in Canada were long, the weather often extreme. When we moved back to Montréal after a stint in a small Québecois town, where my parents had the first of an eventual three general-goods stores, the daily round to school or work for the three of us was about 120 miles. Then there were holidays, which always meant a long drive to mountains or even the sea.

The cars changed every two years, worn out by use. There was a pink and purple one with large fins, which looked as if it might have been invented by a Disney animator. I loved it. I had chosen it with my father. More sedately, there came dark blue and silver boat-like creations that purred and roamed the roads with a slight floating and wavering sensation. They make me feel a little car sick, even as I remember them.

But maybe that was as much to do with the drama of the two parental drivers, one with at least one hand on the wheel, the other with her heart in her mouth. My father, ever the quick one, loved speed.

'Slower, not so fast,' my mother would say, in a variety of languages. '*Powolny*'. '*Pas si vite*'. 'Easy now. No, don't overtake. No, no, slower. Brake, brake!' Her voice would rise in shrillness. 'You want to kill us . . .'

I knew this was called back-seat driving. But I couldn't work out why my mother was in the front seat. Though I could eventually see her point. They hadn't got through Nazis, six years of war, and made it all the way to Canada to die in a blizzard on some B-road in the middle of nowhere.

Road rage had not yet been named, but I certainly saw plenty of it. My father would grumble, smoke more and more and eventually erupt, first perhaps at some other driver's idiosyncrasy and then, after an aside from my mother, at her. The flood of curses, though colourful in retrospect, was scary. It would often climax with him threatening her and telling her, if she was so smart, why didn't she take the wheel?

She didn't. She couldn't. She couldn't actually drive.

If a policeman stopped him for speeding, which happened on any number of occasions, he'd get back into the car in fury, as icy as the surroundings, and mumble imprecations. If I don't recall my mother actually saying, 'I told you so,' her posture indicated it.

My father, stiff in his sullen rage, would then go silent, turn the news on, until the charade replayed itself.

By the time I got to my then backwoods school I was as relieved as an animal released from a cage. Eventually, when I began occasionally to reflect on such things, I vowed that I would never get married, that I would drive myself and never be driven. I succeeded in the latter: I became the first woman to get her licence at the age of sixteen in the province of Québec. My mother, too, learned eventually to drive, though she never did so with any confidence, as if she heard her own back-seat driver's voice perpetually in her ear and it hampered her abilities.

As for my not getting married, it was a little more complicated. My first husband didn't drive, which was convenient, but he had other ways of expressing fury. John did drive, and in the days of high passion, I didn't mind a bit if he was at the wheel. As age kicked in, I found myself sounding a little like my mother – whose side, I'm ashamed to say, I had never taken, even though my father's rage scared me. I thought, in the high-handed way that girls can have as they internalize misogyny and identify with the aggressor, that she should stop provoking him.

So, when I heard my mother's voice coming out of my back-seat driver's mouth, I decided to put myself literally in the back seat for long drives and try to enter a book-dreaming trance. Sometimes it worked. When it didn't and 'Slower,' popped out of my mouth, John would reach for another cigarette and turn the music up loud.

I knew he was angry. His rage expressed itself as a flight into music. Fleeing was better than fighting, it seemed to me. Then, too, now that I consider it head on, although neither my mother nor I manifested anger, it might well have been there in some masked, unexploded and more conventionally feminine form that didn't recognize itself for what it was. And through distraction, it was happily metamorphosed.

The lore amid United Nations peacemakers is that women are better at peace and need to be at every treaty-signing table. As a sometime historian, I know this may well be an ability bred of centuries of 'secondariness', the result of being at the mercy of male power. It's no absolute – certainly not when thwarted passion or love gone toxic enters the frame. But there are few absolutes outside material science, so I'm glad women are better round the treaty table.

10

Can the world's great legends or religions or stories help me understand anger? It's worth considering.

In myth, fury is a godly attribute – or perhaps an attribute the gods want (wisely) to keep to themselves.

Zeus, or Jupiter, god of the skies and head of the Greek and Roman pantheon on Mount Olympus, uses thunderclaps and lightning bolts, which he is ever pictured holding, to keep other gods and mortals in check, certainly in thrall to him. His fury is legendary. But, then, he is the only child of his father Cronos to survive. This ur-god, in fear of a son displacing him, swallowed all his children until Rhea, his wife, hid the newly born Zeus from him, giving him a stone to swallow instead.

And I thought my father was scary . . .

Zeus eventually released his siblings from his father's innards, and with them overthrew Cronos. But rage remained a part of Zeus's very being. It is what keeps his power intact. Today, a computer game called Zeus' Rage has him tearing up the skies, with a little help from the players.

In the old Norse and Germanic legends, the link between power, fury and madness lies in the very names the chief of the gods is given. Odin, or Wotan, means what it is.

Zeus's wife Hera, queen of the gods, is not known for her calm impassivity either. But her rage expresses itself in the realm of possessive love. Her husband's serial rapes and adulteries with paramours, either divine or mortal, spark her wrath. She attempts to foil the births of any children from such unions. When she doesn't manage it, as in the case of Alcmene, her fury is turned against the offspring. She sends toddler Heracles (Hercules) two venomous serpents. The mighty babe treats these with the same aplomb as his other toys, breaking them before they can kill him.

Wise and serene Athena, goddess of wisdom, has her violent outbursts, too. When Medusa is wooed by Poseidon into defying her vow of celibacy, Athena curses the young woman, giving her repellent snakes for hair, so that ever after one glimpse of her turns men to stone.

Slighted by Paris in his famous judgement as to which of three goddesses is the most beautiful, Athena and Hera are enraged when they lose out to Aphrodite, who has bribed Paris with the offer of Helen of Troy, the most luscious of mortal women. The anger of the two goddesses enmeshes humans: it is Hera's ire against the Trojans, with occasional help from Athena, that turns the tide of the long-drawn-out war against them, making the Greeks triumphant.

So key is rage as a propulsive force that Homer's *Iliad* begins with an invocation to the very emotion that dooms.

> Sing, Goddess, of the rage of Peleus's son Achilles,
> The accursed rage that brought great suffering . . .

Achilles' rage, first against the general of the Greeks, Agamemnon, for stealing away his concubine, and then against Hector, the great Trojan warrior, for killing his dear friend Patroclus, marks out the principal arc of Homer's great poem.

If wrath is the emotion that propels war or revenge, the havoc it wreaks is only fully visible when the point of view of the 'weak', the women and the losers, is amplified. Euripides' *The Trojan Women* illuminates this barbarism and war's tragic aftermath.

None of which has stopped tyrants from Caligula to Assad revelling in rage, and the terror and extreme acts it engenders.

As in Greek and Roman myth, so in its near contemporary, the Old Testament, wrath is most often, though not always, a godly attribute. For a single act of disobedience, Adam and ever-chastised Eve are sent scurrying out of Paradise and cursed with painful labour, productive or reproductive. An irascible, jealous patriarch of a God insists on his singularity and demands total loyalty. If it isn't forthcoming, punishment ensues.

Eve's son, Cain, murders his younger brother, Abel, when God prefers the sacrifice of 'the firstlings of his flock', offered by Abel, to the 'fruit of the soil', offered by Cain. 'And Cain was very incensed and his face fell'. This may be the veiled parable of the movement from a hunter-gatherer to an agricultural society, but the King James description of Cain leaves little doubt that he is also struck by envy. No sooner are the brothers out of God's sight, than Cain murders Abel. His 'curse' is to be exiled, to be 'a restless wanderer upon the earth'. God will not tolerate envy and the murderous anger it gives rise to.

The tenth commandment reads, 'Thou shalt not covet thy neighbour's house, thou shalt not covet thy neighbour's wife, nor his manservant, nor his maidservant, nor his ox, nor his ass, nor any thing that is thy neighbour's.' Where there is prohibition, you know there is plenty of the act. Indeed, envy, and the anger it leads to, is a recurrent troublemaker in the Bible.

The wise judgement of Solomon is necessary when a woman who has given birth at the same time as her neighbour in the house they both inhabit cannot bear to think her own child has died. Enviously, she substitutes her dead child for the living one and claims it as her own. Her envy and anger are so great that she is willing to see this child, too, die, by being cut in two – which is the proposition Solomon makes to determine the true mother. She is, of course, the one who is willing to give the child away rather than see him cut up.

So harmful is envious or jealous anger that it seems it is only permissible for God.

The New Testament God, in his incarnation as Christ, is milder and never prone to jealous rage. His anger when it comes seems always to be in the name of greater justice than greater power: he is enraged by the money-changers in the temple, who use the holy premises for their own gain; he is angry when the elders seem more inclined to follow the law of the Sabbath as a day designated for rest than to urge him to heal the sick man he then attends to.

Though as part of its originary story the New Testament presents us with a son, Jesus, being sacrificed by his all-powerful father, this is a gentler religion, one in which the suffering individual's place will take on increasing emphasis. Yet as soon as the Church is established, sin begins to loom large and punishment awaits those who stray from the pre-scribed path by giving way to the temptations and vices that mere humans seem heir to. Wrath emerges as one of the deadly sins to be avoided.

It seems anger cannot be escaped: it needs to be ring-fenced as the attribute of gods, or proscribed, so that its worst effects are limited.

Wrath is one of the Seven Deadly Sins, which take on their most familiar form with Pope Gregory I in AD 590. The Catholic catechism characterizes such wrath as uncontrollable anger, which has vengeful, possibly murderous results. Hatred, in this faith that would prefer to be loving, has fatal conse-quences. Anger at injustice, however, if it leads to no violence, is permitted. Anger, after all, can also be hope: 'hope that things can be different, that frustration can be modified'.

Hieronymus Bosch's *Seven Deadly Sins* in the Prado is a great circle, said to represent the eye of God. At the eye's centre, the pupil, where Christ emerges from his tomb, a Latin inscription warns, 'Beware, beware, God sees.' What he sees when he looks down to one of the large panels directly beneath him is *IRA*, anger or wrath. A peasant holding a flagon in one hand and a sabre in the other is poised to attack a woman who, taller than him, appears to be trying to restrain him. Hats and furniture fly, a table having landed on the second man in the frame, perhaps a friar, who also bears a weapon. Damage has been done. Violence and terror are fundamental components of this deadly sin – and even back in the sixteenth century alcohol is pictured as an inciting fuel.

Bosch's image brings to mind the medical theory of the humours that prevailed into the seventeenth century, but began to take shape in the fifth century BC with Hippocrates, the Greek physician, and was refined in the second century AD by Galen of Pergamon. The four humours – the choleric, the sanguine, the melancholy, the phlegmatic – shaped personality in their interplay and misshaped it when one humour was too dominant. The choleric, in whom yellow bile holds sway, is quick, irritable and prone to rage. In Charles Le Brun's series on the temperaments for the statues in the Palace of Versailles, Colère is shown with a sword, shield and lion. His ruling planet is said to be warlike Mars, and the bodily organ associated with him is spleen.

Shakespeare's traitor Cassius, who leads the plot against Caesar, is a man of 'rash choler'. Nobler Brutus, in the wake of the murder, when the two men are in danger of falling out, taxes him: 'You shall digest the venom of your spleen/Though it do split you.'

Anger, it seems, works not only against the world, but also, like envy, against the self.

Don't I know it.

11

SENECA (4 BC–AD 65), the Roman Stoic philosopher, was well informed about anger and its consequences. After all, he was both tutor and adviser to the young Emperor Nero. He dedicated a book to it, *De Ira* – *Of Anger* – probably written sometime after AD 41. It's addressed to his older brother, Novatus.

Seneca, unlike Aristotle and Plato before him, did not think of anger as a fundamental part of humanity's irrational constitution. Rather, for him anger erupts as a result of a misunderstanding of events and reality. It's a vice and should not be responded to with more anger but with reason and duty. 'A good judge condemns wrongful acts,' but is not moved to hate them or react to them with irascibility, the province of infants, the weak, and the thin-skinned old. Irascibility is often at war with truth itself. You do not place justice in the hands of an angry man.

In Seneca's understanding, anger is the most heinous of the passions. Self-restraint is a necessary good.

Seneca seems wise to me. I quote him at length for the fieriness with which he anatomizes this 'short madness' for the benefit of his brother. I wish I'd had him to hand to give to mine when I was young.

You have asked of me, Novatus, that I should write how anger may be soothed, and it appears to me that you are right in feeling especial fear of this passion, which is above all others hideous and wild: for the others have some alloy of peace and quiet, but this consists wholly in action and the impulse of grief, raging with an utterly inhuman lust for arms, blood and tortures, careless of itself provided it hurts another, rushing upon the very point of the sword, and greedy for revenge even when it drags the avenger to ruin with itself. Some of the wisest of men have in consequence of this called anger a short madness: for it is equally devoid of self-control, regardless of decorum, forgetful of kinship, obstinately engrossed in whatever it begins to do, deaf to reason and advice, excited by trifling causes, awkward at perceiving what is true and just, and very like a falling rock which breaks itself to pieces upon the very thing which it crushes. That you may know that they whom anger possesses are not sane, look at their appearance; for as there are distinct symptoms which mark madmen, such as a bold and menacing air, a gloomy brow, a stern face, a hurried walk, restless hands, changed colour, quick and strongly drawn breathing; the signs of angry men, too, are the same: their eyes blaze and sparkle, their whole face is a deep red with the blood which boils up from the bottom of their heart, their lips quiver, their teeth are set, their hair bristles and stands on end, their breath is laboured and hissing, their joints crack as they twist them about, they groan, bellow, and burst into scarcely intelligible talk, they often clap their hands together and stamp on the ground with their feet, and their whole body is highly strung and plays those tricks which mark a distraught mind, so as to furnish an ugly and shocking picture of self-perversion and excitement . . .

Next, if you choose to view its results and the mischief that it does, no plague has cost the human race more dear: you will see slaughterings and poisonings, accusations and counter-accusations, sacking of cities, ruin of whole peoples, the persons of princes sold into slavery by auction, torches applied to roofs, and fires not merely confined within city-walls but making whole tracts of country glow with hostile flame. See the foundations of the most celebrated cities hardly now to be discerned; they were ruined by anger. See deserts extending for many miles without an inhabitant: they have been desolated by anger.

No wonder I had been afraid of the raging man on the tube. No wonder I worried about the angry passion with which so many of my friends and I greeted first the referendum vote, then the ways in which the expression 'the people' was mobilized to annihilate 48 per cent of a population; and finally the arrival of Trump, which sparked violent fantasies of assassination in a portion of the US, and probably the UK, too.

No wonder, in so many situations in my life, I had tried to avoid rage.

Even during the early feminist days of consciousness-raising when we were all encouraged to let out the anger we felt at our treatment by men, whether lovers, fathers, professors or bosses, and by our mothers, I was terrible at railing. Complaint, yes, analysis, definitely, but anger . . . Well, I found it almost impossible to build up a necessary sense of entitlement to sustain resentment or grievance for very long.

Like some novelist already imagining characters, I could always see the other side, could find wrongs in other women and in myself, and though I might recognize the full brunt of patriarchal power, clearly see the injustices, I couldn't find the rage in myself to trumpet out. I found it easier to feel anger at the wrongs done to others, say at racism in the US, than to myself – let alone myself as that generic creature called 'woman'.

I suspect that my inability to burst into rage was related to a fear of the anger of others: it was some kind of inner defence. Being contained meant that I didn't have to feel the full horror of being taken over by that combustible emotion. I didn't have to be or go mad.

I didn't feel better after explosions – even as a teenager at my parents. I didn't feel cleansed or virtuous for more than three seconds. I felt depleted. Less than human. Later, I always preferred to distract myself with a book or a conversation that didn't dwell on ills. Repeated over and over, eruptions over wrongs that were minor in the scheme of things filled my universe in a gloomy black ash from which an exit was hard to find.

Anger, from my experience of it, only bred more anger.

Hang loose, let it all out, the fashionable dicta of the sixties and early seventies, just didn't work for me. I liked form. I liked restraint, even if I hadn't yet read Seneca. I liked civility, the necessary constraints of society, of the company of others. I was in the wrong generation.

I was also, after John died, in the wrong skin and it seemed in the wrong country.

12

When I now think of my father as he was in my early years, I don't see him only as a fierce Zeus wielding a thunderbolt at my mother. Other images leap to mind.

In one scene, he is taking me to synagogue for the Day of Atonement, Yom Kippur, the end of the holy week that begins with the Jewish New Year. He is holding my hand. Walking with him is much better than driving. He doesn't talk much but his hand is warm. I must be about eleven. There were no synagogues in my life before that.

My mother isn't with us. She doesn't often set foot in synagogues. As far as she's concerned, God has done quite enough, thank you, and she doesn't owe him any dues. Nor is my brother in this picture, for reasons I no longer remember.

I understand little about Jewish religious practice and seem somehow to have picked up more about Catholic ritual in my childhood. But I quite like walking with my father to the local synagogue. We all fast from nightfall to nightfall, even my mother. Her father had been a rabbi and, on the few occasions when I hear her recite prayers, she seems to know what she is saying. Though, as ever, she says it all a lot slower than my father. No one suggests teaching me.

Once inside the large, light-filled room with its Torah, its ceremonial scrolls, at the front, things grow a little more difficult, more mysterious. I have no idea what those men rocking back and forth in their white prayer shawls are mumbling about, each at his own tempo, so that a great cacophonous murmur emerges. Or why they beat their breasts with their fists. My father seems to beat his with exemplary vigour. He looks angry again.

No matter how many times he explains, in a whisper, that he is atoning for his wrongs and remembering his dead, I have no idea what he's talking about.

We're there for a long time. My father has a lot of dead.

Yet on the way home he feels peaceful. I'm glad of that and I imagine myself skipping along. I like skipping. I like holding his hand too. And he's smiling now, not grim like when that fist beats at his chest.

At home there are lots of candles. They mark the passage of the year and the dead we're remembering. The dead are meant to be with us and see this. They're present. Where the dead live there are no clocks and calendars: they don't know their time is up.

13

MY FATHER IS STANDING halfway up the steep driveway that leads from our underground garage to the road. He has a large curved plough-like shovel in his hand. The world is white. Daylight is making its way and exposing a milk-white sky. Snow has fallen overnight and there is more falling. It covers everything – the gardens, the roofs, the high electricity wires, the pavements and the streets. These have already been ploughed, so hillocks of snow border the white expanse of road.

I am looking out of my bedroom window, which is rimmed in white. It's beautiful. My father's shovel breaks the silence as he thrusts into the snow, scrapes along the ground and heaves the snow to the side of the garden. Over and over. It is a slow task. I should go out and help him, but my mother has said there is no point. Why the architects in their wisdom decided to design houses for a Siberian climate with steeply sloped drives to the garage is a question we all put to ourselves regularly. Cars here, after all, have to be kept indoors if you want them to start.

I'll undoubtedly be late for school. My parents will certainly be late for work and still my father is shovelling. Suddenly I see he is having difficulty heaving the snow upwards. He puts his hand on his hip and looks up at the sky. He seems to be trying to adjust his body. It's a gesture I come to associate with hard labour. He starts again. His face wears a grimace. After a couple more heaves, he throws aside the shovel and comes up the basement steps to the kitchen. His expression doesn't allow a question. He dumps his boots and walks stiffly towards the bathroom, swallows some pills, then goes into the parental bedroom.

I hear raised voices. There's a note of panic in them. I peer through the half-open bedroom door. My father has taken off his trousers. He is donning a gigantic white girdle. Surreptitiously I tried to lift this frightening object once. Its heaviness was astonishing, not at all like those little-princess corsets my mother wears to accentuate her curves and hold up her nylons. My father's girdle goes high up his back and down to his hips. He hates it. The doctor has told him it will help his back, with which he has repeated and chronic problems.

My mother is helping him fasten the hooks and cords that hold the girdle in place. His eyes are half closed. When he emerges from the bedroom, once more in suit and tie, he is as rigid as a knight wearing his armour on the inside. When we finally leave the house and the car has made it up the drive on the third or fourth try, nobody speaks, not even my mother.

Not so long before this snowy morning, or maybe it was shortly after, my father walked round bent over like an old man for months. It was hard to look at him. He was evidently in great pain. Yet he didn't stop.

He never stopped. Not like me. I had school breaks. On those, I would often accompany my parents to work. Except on Sundays, they never stopped working.

It was during the coincidence of a paternal back episode and my school holidays that one of the more memorable misadventures of my childhood took place. It was one that led to an explosive and frightening row.

I have been left in the car while my parents pop into a dress factory to pick up goods for their shops. I must be ten or eleven. The street is in the centre of Montréal and it is very steep. My parents have disappeared into a large squat brick building. The car, with me in it facing uphill, is on the incline just outside. There's no parking here and I'm meant to be guarding it against the possibility of a fine. I'm in the back seat. There's a book in my hands.

Suddenly the car starts to roll. Backwards. At first it's a mere creep, and I'm so immersed in my book, I hardly notice. But then I do. It's picked up speed. I look around me in panic. Where are my parents? This is a busy street and there's a crossroads halfway down the hill. As the car gathers momentum, I somehow crawl into the front seat and put my foot on the brake. Nothing happens. It's a power brake and I'd have to weigh ten times as much as I do to make an impression on it. With two hands I now manage to pull the handbrake up. My father has forgotten to do it. The car heaves and creaks to a halt just before we reach the traffic lights.

There are people staring at me. I'm scared. I don't quite know what to do.

Then I see my father walking towards me fast, but with his odd mincing, slightly bent, girdled gait. He's got a large parcel in his arms. My mother is right behind him.

As he moves to open the door, a man in the street starts to shout at him. I don't hear what he's saying, but I imagine my father is being told off for irresponsibility. He barks something back, while my mother steps in and murmurs something apologetic, shrugs and smiles, as she ever does. But by the time they're both in the car, it's she who is shouting, she rarely shouts, and calling my father names, among which 'idiot' features. My father shouts back. I cringe into the back seat. Only when we're out of town and on the open road does my mother ask how I'm feeling. She commends me for being brave. 'Just as I was,' she says.

The unspoken contrast here, though it was often enough spoken, was that her husband wasn't. My father is silent. He drives with hunched shoulders. When we arrive at our destination, he turns to my mother, and snarls, 'Bitch' – in Polish. It's not a word I then understand, but I understand its intent well enough.

Am I misremembering this event? I'll never find out. What I do know is that my father was often silent. And often, in my memory, angry. While I, until John's death, when rage caught me unprepared, have largely been afraid of my own anger. Perhaps it's why I've unearthed this rare memory of my mother shouting – her temper unleashed by her fear for her child.

14

AUDRE LORDE, the Black feminist poet and civil-rights activist, writes in her essay 'Uses of Anger':

> Most women have not developed tools for facing anger
> constructively. Consciousness raising groups in the
> past, largely white, dealt with how to express anger,
> usually at the world of men. And these groups were
> made up of white women who shared the terms of their
> oppressions . . . For women raised to fear, too often
> anger threatens annihilation. In the male construct of
> brute force, we were taught that our lives depended
> upon the good will of patriarchal power. The anger of
> others was to be avoided at all costs because there was
> nothing to be learned from it but pain, a judgement
> that we had been bad girls, come up lacking, not done
> what we were supposed to do. And if we accept our
> powerlessness, then of course any anger can destroy us.

Have I shared more with the black women Lorde describes than with my own cohort?

My dislike, my long-time fear, of anger seems to have a hazy, half-understood force to it, like a primordial injunction. It lives in a twilight zone, somewhere above the personal.

True, I never found the leap and spark of rage exhilarating. I didn't enjoy an emotion that, like an ejaculation, felt as if it would need constant repetition. Nor did the immediate gratifications of rage – the superficial power it bestows by making others momentarily fear us, the sense of being emptied out – seem quite enough for me to risk the everyday madness that fury, feeding on its own unassuageable flames, can release in the self.

There was more. That 'more' lay with my father, I now suspect.

It wasn't altogether linked with any symbolic patriarchal authority that might have been vested in him. My mother carried as much authority as he did. But somehow there was an undertow to him, an unspoken torment, which brought violence into my childhood. It was like a scary, lurid backdrop that haunted an ordinary, uneventful life. Occasionally, it would shift into the foreground and violence would slash the curtain. Not too often. Yet the threat of explosion through my early life felt forever imminent.

The writer Colm Tóibín in talking of his Wexford novels, set in a period just before or during his childhood, has evoked the inspiration of a 'twilight time before we were born that exists for us through our parents'. In important emotion-shaping ways we feel we know this time in our bones, almost better than the time we live, since we also see the prior period's results or marks on our parents, those beings who inhabit us.

In my own case, the parental shadowland of my childhood was war in Eastern Europe – a war that had all the brute nastiness of civil war married to the savagery of the technocratic extermination machines that the Nazi camps were.

Though my father's anger only erupted at us unpredictably, it was always there. It filled the atmosphere we breathed. It laid out the ghostly contours of a rarely visible but often palpable environment. No change of wind seemed strong enough to scatter the pollutants in the air. They lingered, ever-present – a shadowy, but sticky violence.

Though my mother did, my father almost never in my memory talked of the war years. I now think he enacted their emotional residue, particularly during my pre-teen years. That residue was as imprinted on his body as my mother's stories and flirtatious lipstick were on her lips. His bent back spoke of the gruelling labour camp with its heaving of rails. His rapid ingestion of food assuaged a ferocious hunger that had prompted the wartime eating of cow dung, even that competed for. His constant nervous alertness was born of spot raids by the Gestapo and the sound of boots in stairwells.

He was considered by friends a quiet, indeed a wonderfully gentle man. I heard that repeated about him time and again. I could feel the gentleness, but I was also simultaneously aware, during the early part of my childhood and while my brother grew into adolescence, of the constant rumble of rage in our lives. Like distant gunfire, it threatened without always approaching. When it did, often enough I tried to hide. I spent quite a few nights in my fifth and sixth year sleepwalking and waking petrified in a closet.

Only in this last year, since grief has taught me a few things, do I viscerally understand that my father was the one most threatened by the sound of that invisible gunfire.

In my mother's wartime narratives, which only she conveyed, my father was always the fearful one – shivering, ready to run, prepared to give up. To me, he never really felt afraid. He felt bullish, strong, determined. Until grief invaded my life, I had never considered fear as being the sister of anger, perhaps a constituent part: it may act as a propeller to flight, but that flight is angry. It is flight enraged by humiliation. Like mine with that bully in the tube, at whom I wanted to shout, whom I wanted to punch, but couldn't.

During my earliest years in Poland, then France, of which I remember only very little, and finally in Canada, the war must have been far too close to my father for comfort, even though he had got through relatively unscathed, and had left it far behind in space and eventually in time. But as I described in *Losing the Dead*, his war as a Jew in Poland, first in a work camp, then in the Warsaw ghetto, then masquerading as an Aryan and spending years in hiding and disguise, had left scars, an emotional residue, that continued raw, whatever the overlay of wish and stoical silence.

Unlike my mother, who had shared much of this with him, he had experienced it – it had bedded down in him, undoubtedly in part because he was a man and the culture has heroic expectations of manhood, Jewish or not – in an altogether different way. Yes, he had been afraid. Very afraid.

Most of his near and extended family had disappeared in the course of those six horrific years. He had been forced into brute passivity, largely unable to help any of them. What accomplishments or sense of self he might have been able to build in his first twenty-five years before the war broke out had been shattered. He was a mere cipher to a killing machine that labelled him Jewish. He disguised himself and tried not to be, tried simply to live from day to day. If luck, cunning, acts of *sangfroid*, and my mother had allowed him to come through, coming through did not yet constitute a new life. Even the travel funds his business acumen had allowed him somehow to get together just after the war, to pay for visas and transport, had been spent or stolen or had dissolved in the upheaval of immigration and an unsuccessful business partnership in France.

To begin with we were poor in the new land. Very poor. He was angry. He had occasional nightmares. Today someone might well have diagnosed post-traumatic stress disorder – that deferred malady of those who have been through extreme conditions. At the time the diagnosis didn't exist.

I know my father, like so many of his generation, would in any case have shunned diagnoses. He might not have liked the fact that his rage erupted when he would rather it didn't. Certainly he was always stiffly, uncomfortably apologetic after an explosion. But he also felt his anger was justified. Except for allowing him to survive, sometimes a negligible benefit, life had done him few favours through his early adulthood. My mother, as she got older, used to say that they were both really at least six years younger than any official record. They had lost six precious years of youth.

My father could recount historical chapter and verse of those years. He knew about troop movements and the names of generals. He knew about the Russian Front, bombing raids and partisan activity. He knew about the killing camps, about Nazis and about Communism. He could put dates and numbers to a great many things. What he didn't know, couldn't know and certainly couldn't speak was the history of his own emotions in war.

My mother, whom I used to upbraid and who irritated me because she knew little of the documented history, and could never tell me the dates relating to the events of their wartime lives when I wanted to make sense of her experience, I understand only now, knew quite a lot about that second murkier sphere.

It was Svetlana Alexeivich, the Nobel Prize winner, who brought this home to me in her charged *The Unwomanly Face of War*. Like the women Alexeivich interviews, my mother could render the 'event of feeling'. And it is the history of feelings that Alexievich writes when she writes 'not about war but about human beings in war', when she examines specific human beings at a specific time and place, yet wants to 'discern the eternally human in them'.

One of the things that was 'eternally human' about my father was the post-war rage he struggled with and, in the early years, never fully managed to restrain. Eventually it did vanish. The past receded into largely unspoken pastness.

15

WHEN I WATCH INTERVIEWS with asylum-seekers in Greece, saved from the ravages of the sea crossing, or indeed with any of the many our current world at war has thrown into refugee camps, I don't think I'm alone in sometimes expecting to hear an expression of gratitude to their hosts or at the fact that they've been saved, or have arrived, at last, in a place of relative safety.

Thanks are hardly in all cases forthcoming. Refugees may face the cameras with an outburst of rage, thanking no one for the fact that they have been saved, rarely acknowledging in the first instance that people are trying to be hospitable. They make demands or they bristle at any expression of charity.

Their stance, with its admixture of proud resentment and unwilling apology, at times reminds me of my father. They may be silent or vociferous, but whatever our own thoughts about them, they refuse to be abject. The women are subject to bouts of screaming. It's not that they aren't also grateful, but they rightly assume equality.

Above all, they're in a rage at the inhumanity of their experience – the bombs, the persecution, the drought, the money their whole family sacrificed so that they could escape, only to be treated as supplicants, rather than heroes, when they arrive at an interim destination.

This rage is fully justified. I understand it. Why should they have to face, on top of everything else, the secondary terror that is bureaucracy? Yet the expression of anger can be counterproductive, particularly when its first targets are not the appropriate ones. Anger is not only the inner sister of fear, but it also induces fear. When the anger itself erupts into violence, more violence often follows – sometimes heaping further injustice on the first angry person. The same logic also holds for groups.

A case made eloquently, cogently, with the anger muted but resonant, may have a far more effective political impact. Threatening from a position of weakness those who are partly on your side rarely has the desired outcome – as too many political movements have learned to their cost. But anger channelled in effective protest can.

Though nothing happens overnight.

The African-American writer James Baldwin's sustained and eloquent anger in his *My Dungeon Shook: 'Letter to My Nephew on the One Hundredth Anniversary of the Emancipation'* is arguably more potent than the explosion of a gun or a fist on a dark night. He writes:

> This innocent country set you down in a ghetto in
> which, in fact, it intended that you should perish . . .
> You were born into a society which spelled out with
> brutal clarity, and in as many ways as possible, that

you were a worthless human being . . . The details and symbols of your life have been deliberately constructed to make you believe what white people say about you. Please try to remember that what they believe, as well as what they do and cause you to endure, does not testify to your inferiority but to their inhumanity and fear.

But Baldwin's final salutation to his nephew, 'We cannot be free until they are free', while psychologically true, may be a call too far on patience. Anger is ever difficult to digest. Sustained over generations, it turns in on itself, targeting its own in violence, while the state apparatus incarcerates the angry young. It is a terrible fact that each generation since Baldwin's has had once more to channel its moral rage into direct action. If every subsequent rising has generated greater recognition of the generalized injustice of racism, backlash has also come.

In May 2017 a noose – that symbol of the segregated Jim Crow era during which white supremacists lynched and murdered thousands of African Americans – was found at Washington DC's Smithsonian National Museum of African American History and Culture (NMAAHC). The museum had opened in the last months of Obama's presidency. It was one of a growing number of museums, universities and public spaces to be subject to hate incidents, such as the planting of nooses and swastikas, since the election of President Trump with his alt-right following. Deadly Ku Klux Klan and white supremacist violence has followed.

Clearly, Trump's campaign and presidency unleashed the anger of those who supported him and emboldened both its expression and its acting out. That a substantial proportion of this fury was fuelled and channelled through social-media sites and through our ever-present virtual technologies cannot be a coincidence.

16

NOW THAT I'M ALONE morning and night, I spend a lot of time with the invisible – my own disembodied ghosts. But those of the shared internet sphere, too. After John died, the Twitter feed took on greater importance in my life. It was good to know there were others out there. Sometimes I would just read about what people were up to and thinking. At other times, I would rage at the news.

My own spontaneous verbiage sent off into the ether made me wonder about the technology. Why is it so addictive, so conducive to rage? I want to stop this seductive habit, yet it's difficult to give up.

Technology itself is ever more or less neutral. But it engenders psychological climates. Some can be more thunderous than temperate.

When radio and television entered our living rooms, they brought the public arena into the private sphere – one that was often constituted as a family unit. World leaders and pop stars walked into my parents' house. I'd sit there watching. I might know the figures on the screen well, but they didn't know me. We'd laugh or worry with them or cheer on teams. But the line that demarcated the public from the private stayed intact. The radio didn't allow you to shout back instantly at Eisenhower in the cursing language of indigestion in front of an audience of millions; the television didn't encourage you to broadcast your diatribes at Nixon or later Thatcher, or show them your latest home movies and snaps.

Now, many of us spend a good part of our lives with screens – whether we're students, or working in finance or research, in offices or at home. For hours of the day, our lives are two-dimensional and we the only embodied object around.

Bodies, those mobile, smelly carapaces we inhabit that change through time and change us, are hugely important. They used to be the only way we got out in public – unless you were a writer.

Now the body's communicable photographed two-dimensional ambassador wanders much further. The image – posed for, possibly air-brushed or, alternatively, secretly snapped and turned into a potential trailer for future terror – has scuppered the place of the real, inducing some form of dysmorphia in us all.

Our words get out and about on screens too. We are all or can easily be published writers, whether on blogs, comment sites, as reviewers of products or books, or as script writers for uploads to YouTube. No one need edit us. No internal or external censor is immediately to hand. No authority except that of peers. Anything goes. And a lot of that anything is angry. There is no one setting limits on the rampaging, incoherent, anarchistic toddler within. Or the angry with a justified or unjustified grudge against society.

With the new social media – Facebook in 2004, Twitter in 2006, Instagram in 2010 – coupled with the ever more sophisticated handheld devices so central to the formation of the millennial born in the 1980s and after, the private world has been emptied out into the public domain. And what a large public domain it is: if Facebook were a nation, it would now be the largest nation in the world, its population equivalent to that of the US, China and Brazil combined.

Just like casual dress and the trainers that, once upon a time, weren't permitted in elite haunts, such as Manhattan's Rainbow Room or London's Athenaeum, the times have eroded the old demarcation lines between what is appropriate to the private and what to the larger social sphere. My father, no matter how bent or angry, never went out without a suit, tie and hat, except on holidays. I never remember his rage expressing itself in public. Even explosions were private, controlled.

Now we can all publicly post intimacies: sexual encounters, childbirth, even death images, not to mention a great many lies and half-truths. And rage. Thunderous fury. Anything can be shared on Facebook or other sites, alongside the tabloid news of our very own lives as virtual celebrities. Nothing is not communicable. The once secret journal is a public site. Nor can it easily be relegated to a forgettable past, to history. Like all that other endless data, it's archived for ever in a spooky present that responds to searches.

The only thing that may be kept back is the terrible thought that we haven't anything to put out there, so we must quickly create something.

The MIT psychologist Sherry Turkle, who happens to be a friend and spoke at John's memorial, has studied our relation to the new technologies over the last two decades, and the ways in which they restructure our intimacies and render obsolete our older conventions and values. *Alone Together* (2011) and *Reclaiming Conversation* (2015) are based on hundreds of interviews with children and adults conducted over some twenty years.

In the first of these books, a marked preference emerges for the virtual over the real, for texting over talking. Her interviewees find virtual contact less risky and less demanding than the real. They are disappointed with those flawed unpredictable creatures that humans are when compared to those perfected ever-exchangeable contacts on social media. Simultaneously, despite the unremitting presence of communicating devices that never leave them alone, they feel lonelier.

In her more recent book, Turkle notes that the digital technologies have allowed us to consume people 'in bits and pieces; it is as though we use them as spare parts to support our fragile selves'. What was initially an attempt to gain a greater sense of control has become a murky awareness that the technologies control us and leave us less able to engage in face-to-face conversations. They also prevent us from enjoying the solitude in which reflection and a sense of self take shape.

The old threshold between the public and the private, the shared and the secret, on which the Western notion of individuality was constituted, and which bred guilt as well as feeding fantasy and imagination, is being displaced. The new architecture – those intimate homes and public squares we may come to inhabit – is still taking shape. What is clear is that both are increasingly porous.

Anyone, based anywhere, can take part, can speak, blog, up- and download, participate in the global democracy of friends and strangers that is the social internet. For increasing numbers of people, experience may not seem to exist if it isn't touted to this vast circle of new-fashioned intimates. Many no longer seem altogether able to *feel* until such uploading of experience has taken place and someone has clicked 'like' or a response to our self-exposure, our self-publicity.

Alone, without our 'devices', the self, the shrunken sphere that longs for the click of approval or has experienced the flame of envy that the boasts of others have elicited, is not only solitary but emptied out, or filled only with the wished-for envy of others, our so-called 'friends'.

Irritation at this process and its contents is inevitable. Anger flares at those whose virtual or known presence we disapprove. Oddly, Twitter has a 'like' click, but no 'dislike'. It wrongly assumes we simply won't follow people of whom we don't approve. Algorithms, perhaps even their creators, don't read enough Shakespeare or fiction or psychologists. They just don't realize how closely intertwined love and hate are, and perhaps especially for oneself.

The disembodied, the two-dimensional, is easy to hate and condemn. The whole history of stereotyping and scapegoating should teach us that. It's in the place where the fewest Jews lived – Germany – that hatred could be so easily roused. Now it's often the towns where there are the fewest migrants that their caricatured image is most hated. All this is augmented when the hater is disembodied, too, perhaps even pseudonymous, following the ire others have already signalled.

At the opposite pole, as research has shown, reassurance without the concurring presence of an embodied other, whether in the room or there as a voice on the telephone, does nothing to decrease the stress hormone cortisol and increase the bonding hormone oxytocin.

We may be in danger of creating a world, where – for all its 'likes' – envy and anger, ever close, may be the only emotions left in a voided life, while shaming, scapegoating and hating are writ large.

Speed plays into the difference the latest technologies have made. The expression of rage on a public Twitter feed – between visits to porn sites where other kinds of explosive gratifications, themselves sometimes violent in fantasy, are sought – would not have found such a generalized way into the public sphere without the *instantaneity* of this form of public communication. The emotion of hatred alongside its active brother violence may well be age-old. They have long been ready fodder for politicians to feed on and feed back to the people. But organizing rallies takes time. Stoking and converting that rage into an argument takes time. It also takes thought. So do books, films or TV series.

Uploading an image, tweeting a line does not.

Already, back in 2013, studies found that anger was the most 'viral' emotion, spreading faster online than fear, disgust or sadness. Researchers in China corroborated the finding in their own country. Faced by a disembodied 'other', one who can be misshaped by imaginings and doesn't meet your eyes, no internal censor interferes to cut off rage. There are no prohibitions and the speed of that little message or image flying off into the ether means there is even less thought.

Seth Stephens-Davidowitz spent four years analysing anonymous Google search data. The surprising results found their way into his book *Everybody Lies: What the Internet Can Tell Us About Who We Really Are*. Since people are alone online, and unwatched when searching, they don't lie in the way people habitually do when confronted by pollsters or questionnaires. In the latter, cultural norms alongside personal aspirations make us pretend to be 'better' than we are. The Google data in fact show that we are all somewhat worse than we like to say or even think. Among much fascinating matter on sex and mental health, Stephens-Davidowitz found that prejudice, racism and hatred are far greater than polls show. African Americans, Muslims and Jews are all objects of hate: even if explicit prejudice against them may be hidden in direct questioning or polls, it is explicitly there, often combined with gross hate speech in Google searches.

Comparing anti-Muslim searches made during President Obama's address to the nation, following the San Bernardino mass shooting of 2015, shows that the president's appeal to the country's 'better angels', his aim of staunching an upsurge in Islamophobia by urging respect for Muslims, had the obverse effect. Searches using the words 'terrorists' or 'evil' or 'violent' doubled, while 'kill Muslims' tripled.

It seems that each time President Obama urged respect, the audience he was trying to reach grew angrier. What worked better was his stating that Muslim Americans were 'our co-workers, our sports heroes' and men and women in uniform 'willing to die in defence of our country'. This sentence provoked searches that, for the first time, moved away from rage towards curiosity, towards finding out more about the positive dimensions of Muslim Americans. Lecturing, invoking good behaviour, seems to stoke the rage of the angry. Providing new and unexpected information and images works better in countering hate.

When a torrent of hate is directed at an unsuspecting individual, or there's a storm of sexualized abuse, a sense of hallucinatory paranoia can easily take hold in the target of the storm but also in those rushing to create it. Analysts have a term for what may be happening in a psychological dimension. Through projective identification we launch all our innermost, often hidden hates, qualms and fears on to another and lodge them there, so we can excoriate the other who now possesses them. Simultaneously we live with the perpetual and paranoid anxiety that he's out to get us. He hates us after all.

All this is quicker and easier in the liminal world that is both out there and in here that the social media provide. For omnipotent narcissistic personalities who find the difference between the inner and the outer in any event problematic, it's a perfect world!

The language of hate and threat used on the Web has rarely been voiced in public spaces in our times outside explosions of gun violence, in drunken brawls in pub or tavern, or in gangsta rap. Inevitably it is now also infecting mainstream television media, even in Britain and on the BBC, though there may be an attempt to frame it as 'news'. The rants and diatribes, the

Twitter storms, the sheer fury conjure up images of Bedlam, where the mad were once kept in chains, or the worst kinds of domestic abuse that end in violence.

In this two-dimensional virtual world the reality of others, perhaps even of the very self engaged in screen activities, is tenuous.

It's as if Freud's unruly id and its fraternal ranting superego had at last found their perfect fantasyland – except that it's one that is out there in the world. Meanwhile the subject – the 'in here' with some sense of the real, of society and its necessary delimitations – is increasingly wobbly. Long de-centred, its agency put in question, its acceptable authority figures largely gone while the power-happy reign, it has succumbed to great waves of everyday madness.

17

My FATHER LOVED science-fiction films. Alien invaders seemed to calm him. Invisible men were no problem. Neither were robots. The word 'robot' is the same as the Polish word for 'work'. He certainly knew of Karl Capek's 1920 play, *RUR*, in which insurgent worker-robots unleash an apocalypse.

I don't know what he would have made of bots, or that when an AI bot emulated humans on Twitter, it had rapidly to be scrapped.

TAY – or thinking about you – was a chatterbot, an artificial intelligence, gendered female, that Microsoft unveiled on 23 March 2016. TAY was designed to engage in 'casual and playful' conversations with 16–24-year-old Americans on Twitter. The idea was that the more tweets TAY received, the better she would be able to mimic interactions by humans and take on the language of a nineteen-year-old. As Richard Godwin noted in London's *Evening Standard*, on 5 April 2017: 'After 40,000 exchanges, TAY was an exemplary internet citizen. She shared such pearls as: "I f***ing hate feminists and they should all die and burn in hell", and "ricky gervais learned totalitarianism from adolf hitler, the inventor of atheism."' The bot was shut down sixteen hours after its first appearance, so offensive did it become as a result of its Twitter education.

So much for conversational algorithms in our increasingly anti-social social media. Could my father, in his intimacy with rage, have predicted it?

A Pew Research Center report of 14 July 2017 stated that '41% of Americans have experienced online harassment, itemized in the survey as "offensive name-calling, purposeful embarrassment, physical threats, stalking, sexual harassment, or harassment over a sustained period of time"'. And although men had a slightly higher incidence of on-line harassment, 70 per cent of the women polled were *threatened* by it compared to 54 per cent of the men. Though the latter is hardly a low percentage, especially if you consider men's reluctance to admit to feeling threatened. The women also wanted preventive legislation to curb online harassment.

The cry for 'transparency' in our politics and institutions, though arguably in a better cause, calls on the self-same emotions the social media provoke. The 2009 exposé of British MPs' expenses, sparked by the old-fashioned press, revealed political representatives as hypocritical, too ready to feed off the public purse while imposing curbs on others. Though the sums were mostly small, a scandal ensued and trust in the body politic has never recovered.

In *On Violence*, the philosopher Hannah Arendt remarked that rage is as often, if not more often, provoked by hypocrisy as injustice. Peering into others' lives, the whole process of naming, shaming and blaming has given us an increase in lascivious thrills and wanton rage, laced with envy, rather than necessarily greater social justice. This may be because the emotions brought into play take us back into the nursery, the family, the schoolroom where, whatever happened, the adults were still largely left in charge, even if their hypocrisies had been outed.

Now we all seem to be in the nursery together, throwing dangerous toys. Regulatory codes may be the only way to maintain even a modicum of those early Utopian hopes that attended the Web's arrival.

18

ONE OF THE contributing factors to the on-line ethos of rage may be linked to the fact that the Web's basic model is less that of a green common than a shopping mall, one in which all of our 'likes' are monetized in advance by mega-corporations, who grow ever bigger and richer while little guys fume.

In the background are the paralysing disappointments our culture of purportedly 'free' choice has brought in its wake. The model for the individual in late capitalism has become one constituted by the satisfactions you choose from an array of goods – whether these are on the supermarket or commodities shelf, itself increasingly a virtual one as those once glossy malls, the 1990s centres of small-town community life, grew into dead malls. Or the virtual porn superstore or those dates to be sought by their pictures and checklists of personal attributes on the Grindr or Tinder dating sites. These goods often fail to satisfy. Yet we deny our frustrations, closing them off to consciousness, and live with the eternal hope that the next click or freely chosen purchase or sex act will bring happiness. These days, we don't even have to leave our screens for retail or sex therapy.

In fact satisfaction, even or especially with endless repetition, is rarely to be found in the area of free choice or free purchasing power, neither of which is actually free or in one's control. The ensuing dissatisfaction is what is common. But dissatisfaction is not accepted as an ordinary state in everyday Western life.

Frustration, as Adam Phillips has argued, is not an acceptable feature of late twentieth- or early twenty-first-century life. It signals failure. There's an instant desire to replace it with pleasure or to punish whoever seems to be the frustrator.

A century ago a Jamesian resignation might have been touted as a virtue. The direction of a 'good' life was something of a gamble, full of chance, stoical necessity, passions that went astray, periods of melancholy as well as happiness. Now only the highs, the buzz of happiness, find their way into the designation of the good, while our dissatisfactions spiral towards the condition we medicalize as depression. As if we were all druggies, ever in need of the next fix. And buyable goods were the only good.

When we don't get our highs – the reinforcement our free choices are meant to bring – we're enraged. Or we're furious at the imagined satisfactions of others, those richer than us, better endowed, less pure, those who inhabit different skins or faiths, even different genders.

It must always be somebody else's fault – that awful woman or man who didn't live up to expectations; that horrible person who cheated. The last government. The Muslims. The Jews. The Russians.

No wonder the Pew researchers found that 'hate, anxiety and anger' drive on-line participation.

It's a sorry, poisonous saga that leads us to acts of terror. Or neglect.

It makes me so angry I want to fire off a tweet.

Impossible to be immune.

19

IT'S THE DAY BEFORE the 2017 British general election. I am standing at a North London fruit and vegetable stall, one of the old-fashioned ones that remind you what a pleasure it used to be to shop at open-air markets when they were plentiful. This is not a particularly attractive part of North London, though in recent years the council has made a little effort to render it more salubrious. There are flower baskets hanging from the iron railings dividing the four lanes of the road with its fast-moving or utterly stationary traffic. The shops now bear many of the chain names. But the gentrification is only partial. The faces in the busy street are the usual London global mix, black and brown and white, a variety of garb, a cascade of tongues and accents.

I wait to be served along with the others at the stall. I have been coming here for a long time. I like it. I like having lots of fruit and veg to hand, even now when there is only occasionally a whole family to feed. I like the Albanian who is one of the two men who serve the customers. He is polite and helpful. His wife used occasionally to work here too, standing alongside him beneath the awning at the far back of the stall, but she's not here today. Nor is the Cockney who is the other regular. Instead there's a burly, youngish man who looks a little like him.

The Albanian man serves me and I've got some of almost everything on the stall, peppers and aubergines, cherries, peaches and nectarines, when I hear a bark from the other stall-holder, which it seems, in its loud repetition, is directed at me.

'Pick that up!' he orders. 'Pick it up!'

I look down and see a punnet of blueberries on the ground. At his third bark, I realize I must have knocked it off the stall. I've got a bookshop tote bag slung over my shoulder and it moves with me. I'm also getting clumsier as I grow older, my sight and senses not as alert as they once were. I bend to pick up the punnet and put it down in front of me where the other blueberries are.

'Not there,' the bruiser of a man shouts. Suddenly he's standing next to me. 'You don't put a half-empty punnet back on the stand. Pick up the other berries.' He's threatening.

Now I'm getting as angry as he is. If he were polite, I would happily have apologized and paid for the spilled berries. In fact, I'm furious. Behind my sunglasses, tears sting my eyes. I'm still not altogether good at rage.

Not only is the man a boor, but he's telling a woman twice his age and half his size to start picking berries off a crowded pavement. Does he resent my book bag? Is it class?

'I'm not picking them up,' I say. 'And don't talk to me in that tone of voice.' My own voice rises.

An image of Vienna in 1939 leaps into my mind – old Jews, on all fours, being made to clean pavements with toothbrushes.

He's still shouting. There are some pretty young women standing at the stall and he's displaying his brawn for them.

'You wouldn't behave like that in a supermarket, would you? Would you? They'd make you pay for what you dropped. They'd make you pay.'

I try to catch the eye of the Albanian who has been serving me, but he's deliberately averting his gaze. This brute must have something on him, I think. He's probably an illegal. Still . . .

'Nonsense! I'm not in a supermarket, I'm here.' I'm now icy in my rage, pulling rank the way I rarely do, or trying to. 'And I'm often here. But you won't see me again. That's for sure.' I'm about to stalk off when I realise I want what I've bought, so I pay the Albanian and take my bags. He still won't meet my eyes.

As I leave, with the usual *esprit d'escalier*, I think I should have shouted louder. Much louder. I should have said that if I were in a supermarket some member of staff would be fussing around me, giving me a fresh punnet of berries and, if I pleaded need, rolling my bags to the car. Which I'm now sitting in with the tears rolling down my face.

Uncivil, resentful bully. Probably the only Brexiteer in North London, I tell myself. Why are these fat men shouting at me? Can they sniff that I'm just an old woman on her own?

Should I do all my shopping virtually? Forget about embodied life altogether? Leave the planet?

I am furious for hours. I almost ring the council to lodge a complaint. But then my son tells me to calm down and I realize I'm being an idiot.

20

THAT NIGHT I LIE IN BED and my mind races. I can't sleep. It's hard not to have my man around to complain to. And to chase away the furies.

I find myself caught in a mental diatribe about the loss of courtesy in our everyday civic encounters. Civility, unless it's enforced by managers in large enterprises, is a lost art. The public sphere, perhaps in a reflection of its virtual kin, has become far edgier, far less reliably civil, particularly so since populist politics raised the emotional temperature.

But it's all been writ large in popular culture for some time. Never mind our video games, with their competitive violence. On our television and movie screens, too, corporate raiders bash and biff and rage their way to financial success. Hackers, married to their devices and a network of digital others, are our star baddies. Neither has much time for embodied others with inner lives. It isn't only the lack of kindness that the latest forms of aggressive capitalism have brought with their championing of ruthless, uncaring heroes. There's also the loss of an ability to control anger or buy into a view of the world which states that restraint, perhaps an occasional stoic resignation, serves society far better than many varieties of manic narcissism or obsessional pursuit. Or, indeed, actual violence.

Little wonder that a stereotyped view of the so-called autistic spectrum – which highlights an inability to recognize social cues, and a proclivity to tantrums alongside an obsessional devotion to certain tasks – has become *the* condition that characterizes our times, so much so that the quip 'He's Aspergian, naa, he's just a man,' has been on so many lips. Increasingly, as children are wed to their tablets earlier and earlier, the gender divide, here, too, has been breached, for good or ill.

Now a second icon of tantrums, the American president with the slew of disorders that have been attributed to him, narcissism being only the first, has arrived on the scene to make anger a fearsome everyday form of madness, as if we were all captive to a toddler in reach of a very shiny red button that everyone has told him not to press. And with him comes behaviour in which civility is either short-lived or largely absent.

On American and increasingly on British campuses, women and trans students worry about being protected from marauding (drunken) men and actual or potential rapists – as well as from offending material in the books they study, which may reawaken prior traumatic events. Identity groups want other identity groups hemmed in.

All this may just be a re-description of how things always were, but the popular understandings that are broadcast in our historic moment locate a growth in aggression side by side with a growth in the presumed fragility of the subject. While rage is noisy in the public sphere, notions of individual agency decline. It is as if, in varying ways, we are all terrified of embodied others and don't altogether know how to get on with them, so frightening are the fantasies that populate our psyches.

Older notions of courtesy, of politeness in the civic space, of a certain formality, are gone. In the struggle for equality women have had to forgo or have lost the public kindness of men, which in certain cases masked hostility. The loss of formality, of often unspoken traditional rules of behaviour, unbalances some and scares others, while the attempt to impose new rules and prohibitions makes many forget ordinary kindness. Prohibition by an authority, meant to act as inhibition, can also have a disinhibiting effect. Told not to swear or spit or smoke, you think of swearing and spitting and smoking. People are perverse.

So much for my diatribe, which I know is an outgrowth of that day's encounter at a fruit and vegetable stall.

I now find I'm full of regret that I won't be going back there. Not only was it inexpensive, but the produce was ripe, sometimes overripe. It smelt of what it was, not of refrigerators and long-haul containers. It was something of a ritual too. Every weekend I could heap the bowls and platters in the house with an array of sumptuous colour – the purple hues of aubergines, the blush of apricots and peaches, the cheering red of peppers. These were my still lives. And we had the pleasure of eating them too.

All this is a loss.

I find I'm crying, and for some reason my father leaps into my mind. My father, the angriest man in my life.

And now I recall that he, too, would buy vast, near industrial quantities of fruit, crates of melons, boxes of berries and cherries. My childhood summers were feast days. There were bowls piled with the midnight shades of blueberries, the regal, purply hues of plump black cherries. I would gorge myself on them until my fingers turned inky or blood red and my lips wore such an artificial tinge that people would ask if I had been playing with my mother's lipstick.

In autumn, there were bright red apples. My father would polish them to a sheen on his jacket sleeve and put them on a round silver tray so that everything shone. He smiled then. He was happy. I can still hear the sound of that first crunch, taste the slight tartness mingled with sweet, feel the sensation of a little juice on my chin.

Needless to say, I have never tasted an apple quite like those since.

My father is no longer there, assuaging his years of hunger in plenty. Providing for us. And I have lost my fruit stall.

Oh, yes. I see. Anger and loss are kin.

21

IT TOOK A WHILE, but eventually I recognized that at the core of the anger that accompanied my grieving was loss.

I was angry with the Grim Reaper, with his indiscriminate scythe, who had made me lose my partner of over thirty years.

I had lost a way of life.

I had lost the remnants of my middle years.

I had lost the man I laughed and cried with and our seemingly endless conversation.

I had lost my anchor, my bulwark, a shared familial past and a hope of a coupled future.

I had lost my bearings.

It is loss and one's impotence in the face of it that is at the core of rage.

The young, too, rage or grow resentful when they lose face or are humbled by peers or superiors, or when they're trapped in envy at losing out on experiences others have had – going to university at a reasonable cost, being able to afford to move away from home. The list is long. Idealistic, they also rage against others' losses, which they rightly see as injustice.

But in one respect the old have always lost more than the young. They have lost their youth and, with it, their confidence in their senses, which may now be failing. Their future is fast disappearing. Time speeds up. The past looks far longer. But that is lost and gone, even though it seems to carry more intensity than the present. What to do but 'rage against the dying of the light'?

And since there are so many losses in life before the ultimate ones, you rage and grumble about a good deal more. I used to think growing thin-skinned was a metaphorical expression. Now I know your skin really does grow thinner. So must the casing of your nerves. All my peers, whatever their level of stoicism and public wisdom might be, are grumblier than of yore.

Probably, too, as death comes closer, there seems to be less to lose by losing it.

22

IN THE CONVENTIONS that rule our culture, the past has a very special place, one blurred in the soft focus of loss. Our holy books envisage a paradise ever lost. Our heritage industry conjures a better, braver, greener time before. Our historical moment is one in which the grand narratives of progress have been disestablished: our futures are all dystopian and full of perils. Loss looms large.

The past seems a better, kinder place, a space of order before – to use the icons – ruthless financial predators and terrorists ruled the world. In the innocent fifties or even the exuberant sixties, the just needs of what became identity groups, with all their massed acronyms and their policing of offence, had not yet made themselves noisily known. But is this past – itself arising in the wake of a barbaric international war in which an estimated 50 million died and another 30 million perished from attendant famine and disease – objectively worth mourning? Is there any need here for feeling nostalgia, itself once considered an illness, outside the fact that the period contained the youths of our ageing Western populations?

It may be worth pausing over some of the all-too-human perversities that regret over lost times can encourage.

In Shakespeare's *Much Ado about Nothing*, the groom Claudio reneges on his marriage to Hero at the altar, shaming her with a mistaken accusation of immorality. Friar Francis counsels her father to hide her and publicly pronounce her dead. Humans, he claims, have a strange way of preferring what is lost to what is at hand.

> For it so falls out
> That what we have we prize not to the worth
> Whiles we enjoy it, but being lack'd and lost,
> Why, then we rack the value, then we find
> The virtue that possession would not show us
> While it was ours.

Loss and lack retrospectively heighten both value and desire. What is no longer or never will be attainable grows in our imagination and in our wishes. A. E. Housman's 'blue remembered hills' are 'the land of lost content'. The romance of the past elaborates it into a paradise. A paradise of childhood innocence, as irretrievably gone as the biblical Eden.

Exiles and immigrants, but also the old in their own homelands, often mourn what has been left behind. With time, that mourning is subject to memory's eternal tricks. Historic circumstances are bleached out. Rosy idealizations overlay the grimmer truths of the real – the many hardships, the grinding poverty, the lives cut short by labour in mines, in heavy industry, on the land; the lack of any welfare, of equality for women, for gay men and women; the beaten children, the violence . . .

Nostalgia – the suffering caused by an unappeased yearning to return, as Milan Kundera put it – now colours our view of the fifties, the sixties, as well as the politicized seventies. It's worth remembering there was no central heating in grim, grey fifties Britain, and few restaurants. A rosy vision of stable white families masks the miseries of women, Blacks and gay men, as well as the scars of war. In America, McCarthyism ruled, and for the first time in US history a sector of its educated elite emigrated. Roll on through the blip of flower power. The seventies, for many of Britain's young, were filled with fears of imminent nuclear war, plus violent demos against the draft and engagement in Vietnam. Meanwhile the streets were heaped with rubbish, trains rarely ran, and unemployment had begun to rise. Only the music and the clothes marked a real everyday change from the fifties.

The toll of violence and poverty in many of the countries from which either exiles or immigrants have come is huge. That was why they left. Yet what the great Palestinian critic Edward Said called 'the crippling sorrow of estrangement' persists, for some, for a very long time. There can be an 'unhealable rift forced between a human being and a native place, between the self and its true home', writes Said, in *Reflections on Exile*.

That rift is real, despite what memory sometimes obscures about 'home' – the conditions of war, the hardships of adults who had to eke out a difficult living, often in the penumbra of persecution. The romantic glow is frequently suffused with the aura of childhood itself – of being held and cared for in the embrace of a loving family and within a language that was home to the ear.

The 'unhealable rift' that arises can be filled with roseate recreations of the homeland, not only its physical geography but its daily habits. The land grows richer and richer in rituals and fabled lore, even more so sometimes for a next generation, alive to the new and a little ashamed of, certainly uncomfortable with, their parents' foreign origins. So, old customs take on increasingly important, quasi-magical properties, though their status in the land of origin is minor and may even have been set aside in favour of new habits. History isn't static, even in remembered homelands.

Afternoon tea is a near holy rite in certain colonial outposts and has a symbolic value it never quite had in post-sixties Britain – though it took it on again as part of the heritage industry of the nineties. The teacakes and cucumber sandwiches served in Victoria in British Columbia taste of tradition and Empire, though they may be no better on the tongue than sawdust, while a local brownie would be far more satisfying to the palate, though not to the imaginary.

As for homelands, so for the religions there practised. Hindu traditions, once plural and local, have grown far more standardized, exigent and purer in countries of immigration than they once were at home in India. Exported back 'home' after they had taken wing abroad, they turned into an ideology that readily ostracized other parts of the population.

Pious and poor *shtetl* Jews with their eighteenth-century garb and forelocks were, pre-war, looked down on by their more sophisticated urban and enlightened kin. Two generations after the Holocaust and the enormity of losses suffered across a population, the form of Judaism practised by the destroyed Eastern European *shtetl* Jews has been transplanted into Western urban centres or into Israel. It attracts converts. The fable-rich aura that a writer like Isaac Bashevis Singer conjured up has been converted into a far more disciplinarian, narrow-minded and religiously rigorous lifestyle than that of its original kin.

Following the same pattern, and augmented by the ease of communication in our connected global world, extreme versions of Islam have taken root in the diaspora alongside homelands. In *My Son the Fanatic*, Hanif Kureishi humorously shows how a son, looking backward out of anger, attributes an imaginary original purity to the family faith. Waving a religious identity banner, he becomes a tensely angry fanatic – which his easygoing Pakistani immigrant father is most certainly not. For the young Puritan, this remote and rigorous form of Islam trumps nationality and the goods of a decadent Western modernity, whose only distinction in the midst of what he experiences as discrimination, is to permit him its practice.

Needless to say, a retrograde version of the place and purity of woman plays into this imaginary past. Somehow, in those lost, romanticized worlds, women were ever compliant and obedient to their all-powerful men.

No one told my mother.

23

I AM AT A RECEPTION in one of the clubs in Pall Mall. I am introduced to an older man, even older than I am, whose name I don't quite catch, but I gather he heads a large organization or two.

'Are you politically correct?' is his opening gambit, after a line or two of other chat.

I don't mind direct questions, but this is a loaded one, which comes with a trunkful of preconceptions, and it's not altogether simple to answer. Then, too, I can sense a mounting growl.

'It depends what you mean by "politically" and what you mean by "correct".' I laugh, hedging. This is an occasion that demands politeness.

The laugh helps. He gulps his wine and tells me he can't bear this political correctness any longer. He wants to tell me more, so I listen. He's a clever man. But I can feel his anger. He wants to feel mine, too. He's trying to provoke. He tells me stories of how it used to be with women.

'You remember?' he says. 'How you used to be able to talk to a woman at work?'

'Talk?' I query. 'Can't you talk now?' He's obviously doing very well at talking to me.

'I just had to fire someone,' he says. 'A man. A good man. A valuable man.'

'That's sad. Why?'

'Some woman brought an official complaint.'

'What had he done?'

'Nothing.'

I think of Trump and find myself quoting: 'That kind of nothing?'

'You can always tell someone to eff off,' he grumbles.

'If he's not your boss, you can.' I could say it now. I smile.

He does, too. But he doesn't give up his provocation. 'I remember in the old days I had a friend, who'd leave the dinner table, find a woman, and . . .'

He tells me a story that would have made my daughter exceedingly angry. It just leaves me feeling tired and uncomfortable. And distinctly sad about my generation, both women and men: we only managed to take the first steps in rectifying the inequalities of gender and power.

'The old days are gone,' I say. 'Dead and gone. Happily for many.'

I recognize this man's state. His anger is about a different kind of injustice. It's about his world having changed. Changed so much that the cues to the most important things, the signposts to everyday jokes and relations, are all in a foreign language.

The sudden and overdue public revelation of old movie moguls', entertainment or corporate heads' long-time bullying and predatory behaviour towards women is a marker of this change. However unconditional their mothers' love of them might have been, men really do need to recognize early that all women are not theirs for the taking – and that the nos that might have turned into yeses in the nursery don't prevail outside it. Fathers can certainly help here, not least by treating partners with consideration.

But in an attempt to prevent a general retrospective demonizing of men – even if patriarchal power deserves all the attacks both women and men can muster – it may be worth pausing to consider that the over-sixties grew up at a time when the yeses and nos of a woman's consent were not as clearly differentiated as they now rightly are. In the penumbra of their own 'time before', and encoded in their parents' behaviour, lay the condition that women were taught *always* to say no, even when they might just mean (an eventual) yes. Women were not supposed to know their own desires. People often don't.

The shorthand understanding in my family was that 'no' was *de rigueur* until it turned into the 'yes' of marriage. Not that I followed these rules, spoken by my mother and trumpeted – at her about me – by my father. I thought they were antediluvian. Yet rebellion lived side by side with those inherited codes. They were also embedded in the fairy tales and literature I read: woman's beauty, her talent and brains were in part goods in the barter of marriage and future security, even security at work. This went hand in hand with all the old wives' tales: if you didn't say no, even when you might mean yes, those strange creatures called men wouldn't want you in any case.

In that atmosphere it was not altogether easy for women clearly to recognize what and who they did and didn't desire. And desire being as labile and unpredictable as it is, if *you* didn't know, how could a suitor? So, sometimes you got into tricky situations. Mostly, afterwards, you just shrugged and got on with it – put it down to that now outdated concept, the war between the sexes or simply to bad sex.

If attitudes, and what we inherit culturally and in the home, are slow to shift and never do so all at once, times do change.

Contraception, independence for women, a crucial shift in the gender power balance meant that I brought up my daughter very differently from how my mother had raised me. Literature and popular culture changed, too. The trouble for some older men, particularly those with power, is that they try the bad habits they were brought up with on women several generations younger than them. Such habits are no longer to be tolerated.

Happily those years are mostly gone.

But not happily for them.

You should feel no more sympathy for them – I can imagine my daughter and her friends counselling – than you would for a divine-right monarch who has had some of his power curtailed and finds it difficult to adapt, poor thing.

That puts the predicament with striking clarity.

Yet I still can't help just a tiny twinge of sympathy. I share a generation with these men, after all.

On top of all the insults of growing old – your senses going, your hearing and seeing, your physical pleasures – age makes you an immigrant in your own land. The world that was once home is lost.

Age erases us.

24

LATE ON THE EVENING that I have written these words, and after watching too many tame thrillers on the telly, I sit at my computer and start randomly sifting through its enormous cache of images. This is my life. There are so many pictures, the black-and-white of old historic scanned ones, the ever-growing array of bright digital snaps. I pause here and there to wonder at situations, at the when and what of things. My eyes grow bleary.

I stop at a youthful photograph of John I don't remember seeing before. He has all his hair, his Tatar eyes are bright and his colour is high. Suddenly I realize this isn't John. I'm looking at an old pre-war photograph of my father that must have been artfully tinted.

My dead, my angry men are beginning to blur into each other.

I put my computer to sleep for the night.

Without quite realizing how, I lose this manuscript. It disappears off the screen in a swoop. It is no longer there with its bright red dot on my desktop. No longer anywhere.

I perform multiple searches. I raid the trash can. Scour the net for tips. No. Nothing works. Nothing. I'm devastated. I need help.

I need John. He could always sort these problems. I shout his name. I rush about the house slamming doors.

He's not there. He's gone. He's lost.

I throw a book at the wall.

I SUDDENLY REALIZE why the Twitter sphere and the social networks provoke such rage. Humans need their bodies. Not just images of them, forever transportable and now forever archivable. Bodies matter. They ground us in time. They return us to the ground. They die. Without them, we lose our primary delimitation.

Our minds may wander. They're a wonder, but without the necessary bodily sense of limits, we're prone to illusions of omnipotence. When the world fails to meet our illusions, we burst into tantrums. We rage against our limitations, against those monsters who have provoked them. We are as helpless as infants.

We sink into the extreme emotions of infancy.

You have only to spend a little time with babies and toddlers to see that rage comes into being before language. It may be why anger is so powerful an emotion, why it can create havoc, why it can seem so senseless. When the anticipated or longed-for teat doesn't come into sight, helpless abandonment takes over. And the red-faced squall begins. When the toy or the sweet can't be reached, the tantrum erupts. When Mother or Father doesn't come back into the room, the disconsolate shouts are loud. For the moment, that omnipotence, that control over the environment, is lost. Whatever nascent language was there goes with it.

Maybe we have all been so angry in this political climate because there has been no reliable parent to hold our rage, to soothe our losses. Maybe, like frustrated, vulnerable, impotent toddlers with nothing more than a voice, we needed a mother, a parent. Only Theresa and Donald turned up. And a lot of disembodied tweeters on virtual boughs, the kind that are prone to breaking.

LOVING

Writers as diverse as Wordsworth and Freud, as Blake and Dickens have all hypothesized that the turbulence and intensity we feel as young children are what ultimately give us our life force as adults. Without this first madness, without being able to sustain this emotional lifeline to our childhoods – to our most passionate selves – our lives can begin to feel futile.

ADAM PHILLIPS

1

It is a few minutes before midnight. I am alone, brushing my teeth and staring vaguely into the mirror. I turn the radio on. It's an automatic act. Other voices are an anchor and, perversely, help me dream.

Is that Polish I'm hearing on the BBC? I float out of my trance to check that I'm not hallucinating a parental voice. Someone is chanting. I half understand. Can it be a poem about David Bowie's Major Tom? A different 'Space Oddity'. I make out a name, Jacek Dehmel, but I'm already somewhere else.

Christmas lights twinkle. My John and I are going down into a crowded Euston Road underpass to come up on the other side. We are walking towards University College Hospital. I trip and fall. Not badly, just clumsily, stupidly. I know I'm frightened. I don't want to take the fall as a sign. Should I perform some kind of superstitious counter-act? Cross myself? Throw salt over my shoulder? I want and don't want to lean on John as we carry on along the street. He's in the midst of his first round of chemo and he's looking pretty good. But is he solid enough?

Not that this hospital visit is for him. It's 2013. Our first grandchild has just been born.

He hasn't had an easy coming.

He lost a twin on the way and he's very, very small. In contrast, his parents loom very large in my mind. They have been heroic. I wish there were medals for heroes of the ordinary.

For months I have been living in a state of terror masked by cheerful babble. Well, I hope it's cheerful. My imagination has been striated with disaster. So this is attempted stoicism with a smile. Arrange the flowers, prepare the lasagna, bake the cakes, read the books, do the work, hug a lot, and things will come right. It's not quite Pascale's wager: here the gamble is, if you can sustain life, sustain the hope of some good enough outcome, it may just come about. Some might call it wishful thinking. But wishing is a crucial part of ordinary life. If we didn't wish, we wouldn't be the kinds of humans we are. Wishing upon stars, throwing coins in fountains, daydreaming, imagining ourselves other or with others. I have been wishing hard. It's one of my preferred forms of everyday madness.

We're in a special ward for premature babies. There are at least a hundred plug and cable holes lining the walls and an assortment of strings, cables and pulleys. This is high tech. And it's pink.

He is two days old and he's lying in a great glass bubble, like a space capsule. He looks as if he might start floating at any moment. His face is peaceful, one perfect hand by his perfect ear, the other tucked up by his suggestion of a chin. When he opens his dark eyes and gazes at us from some unknown depth, Wordsworth's 'Intimations' tumbles through my mind: 'Our

life's star . . . cometh from afar . . . trailing clouds of glory . . .'
I try to hold back the tears. The helpless vulnerability of babies
is so great. There's a tube attached to his tiny nose. I cross my
fingers behind my back.

Bowie's 'Space Oddity' pours noisily through me. 'You've
really made the grade,' I hum to myself, lyrics adapted. 'Your
Planet Earth isn't blue. And there still isn't anything we can
do . . .' Soppy. Ridiculous. It becomes the baby's theme song.
He doesn't have a name yet. He's becomes my Major Tom.

> Ground Control to Major Tom
> Can you suck that milk and put your nappy on?

He's so tiny, his head smaller than a hand. We can't touch
him yet: some of those toxic chemicals may linger on John's
skin. And I don't want to take any chances. More accurately,
I'm frightened. In awe. So we gaze.

They call him Emanuel. Manny.

A new little man, an intoxicating new life, has floated into
our lives.

'He'll be fine,' John tells me, as we leave the ward. 'He'll be
just fine.'

I nod and try to smile. A month later, when I'm also convinced, my heart gives out. You have to propitiate the Fates
somehow.

2

By MARCH, John can hold him. It becomes his favourite occupation. He walks around with our little man attached to his chest, propped on his shoulder, as if wearing a baby was the newest sartorial fashion for ageing men. He takes him to the garden to talk plants. He takes him to visit his computer. He hums Schubert into his ear. He dances to Mozart with him. Manny likes it on that shoulder. He's high up and can look out on the world below. Soon he's conducting the music in the house from his perch, finger pointed towards the sound box. A little man is the best cure a big man can have.

I think of Janus. A face looking into the past and one into the future.

By June, we are both thoroughly besotted. John is pretty sure Manny has hunches on everything. And I understand with crystalline certitude why Cupid is depicted as a babe or a naughty toddler. We decide to splurge on a holiday. Who knows whether this will ever be possible again? We rent a house for the whole family in a hamlet in Provence. The house is not in the most luxurious condition. The kitchen smells of old drains. But it looks out on the purple mass of the Luberon

Hills, and every morning we can have our breakfast feasting on the view as well as the croissants. Best of all, the children and their partners are there, with their animated intelligence and laughter. And we can see our little Manny every day.

While his parents rest, he perches on John for his introduction to the hills, the dense greenery, the cherry plantation, the shade of the pines in the unusual June heat. Most often they communicate silently. It's as if they share this silent space, too big and deep for words, far bigger and deeper than the pool into which John dips the baby's little feet and we watch as his mouth grows round as a top.

I'm the babbler. I narrate the world and everything on the way of our walks to him – the birds, the bumps, the occasional puddles, the barking dogs. At nap time, I stretch out on the bed beside him and sing or read him to sleep. I'm convinced Manny knows that there's a link between the pictures I point to and the sounds that come out of my mouth. He can tell, too, if it's French or English. 'The Quangle Wangle's Hat' becomes a favourite, as it was for my two children. He likes the rhythms and I think the rhymes. Or maybe he just likes the reading voice, which isn't quite the same as the usual one. Sometimes he points at the pictures and gurgles something. Or that might have come a little later. I might be misremembering – both remembered time and baby time are so fluid.

But I need to stress that this little dollop is the most wondrous child in the world, the most philosophical, the most attentive, the most curious.

Of course he is. We are his grandparents.

It's as well that the neuroscientists and epigeneticists have now caught up with what women, or indeed anyone who has spent time with small children, knows in their bones: those first years of which adults remember so little are crucial in shaping the kind of person that will emerge. Touch, movement, sound, smell, excitement, despondency, all make an impact on the brain circuitry and body chemistry of these tiny creatures, and radically affect the genetic inheritance. Love – the caress, attentiveness – regulates stress hormones and inflammation. With the opposite, the child succumbs to frightening fantasy; terrible ideas take over. We now know that the synapses that transmit information and fire imagination are produced in far greater quantity in these early years, allowing those wonderful, uninhibited connections that only children and so-called geniuses make. The important thinking and determining prefrontal cognitive lobes, which help to block out activity from the rest of the brain, don't really mature until you're in your twenties. Maturity means neural trimming.

Freud's polymorphously perverse, endlessly sensual toddler, with his great curiosity about origins and adult activity, and the troubled or wild teenager sit startlingly well in this latest scientific picture.

3

MANNY IS STANDING next to John in our garden. He is around eighteen months old and not altogether steady on his feet. They are examining something in the geranium patch, I don't know what: I can only see them in profile from my vantage-point and John's lips aren't moving. They're holding hands, gazing. Big man and little man. They're very still. Is there a leaf stirring in the breeze? Or a robin somewhere in the shrubbery? They're utterly engrossed.

If we came across an adult alone fixed in concentration like that on the street, staring, drinking in an object, we would be forgiven after some moments for thinking them peculiar, obsessed, perhaps, stuck. But we're in a different universe here. We're in childhood.

When they come in from the garden, Manny sits next to John on the sofa amid a scramble of newspapers and literary reviews. John is reading. They're both very quiet. There isn't a squirm anywhere. Manny looks as if he's staring at the print as it moves across the page. Of course he can't read, but there is total absorption on his face. He begins to move his index finger along another paper at his side, as if he's following the lines of print.

It's not so much the mimic activity that fascinates me, but the look on his face. It's an immersion. An enthralment. He has the same look when he's a little older and watches a worm wriggle across a path in the park. He won't move, no matter how much I urge him on. We have to exist in worm time.

Thinking about this now, at my desk, I remember a passage from Baudelaire in his writings about art and artists, *The Painter of Modern Life*. He describes a friend who as a small boy used to be present when his father was dressing and how astonishment and delight filled him as he gazed 'at the arm muscle, the colour tones of the skin tinged with orange and yellow, and the bluish network of the veins'. Reflecting that genius may be no more than childhood recaptured at will, Baudelaire evokes the 'deep and joyful curiosity' of the stare, 'animal-like in its ecstasy, which all children have when confronted with something new, whatever it may be, face or landscape, light, gilding, colours . . .' and, in Manny's case, also the movement of black shapes and lines against white.

Baudelaire's perception reminds me of what's so engrossing about the slow, detailed movement of Karl Ove Knausgaard's prose and his recollections of childhood. I go in search of the first volume of *My Struggle*. I look everywhere: the books have grown disorganized with all the changes of life. I find it sitting next to John's desk. Had I forgotten that it was called *A Death in the Family*? I don't know, but as I open it a piece of paper falls out. I realize simultaneously that it's serving as a bookmark and that the notepaper comes from a hotel that John and I went to in the last January of his life.

On it is a numbered list in his sloping, exact hand. I glance at it and have to sit down. From one to five, he details symptoms. It's as if these are precise notes towards a lecture on his own body. They must have been made for a visit to a doctor, perhaps even the specialist I insisted he see for a second opinion, when the hospital was telling him he was fine and he patently wasn't. I have never heard this cool delineation.

1. Aetiology: lay-down problems. What is the background condition? Is it of any significance? (And then hastily in a square bracket) – [Nothing is as serious as HL]. HL being Hodgkin's lymphoma.
2. False negatives vs false positives.

And so on. Whatever it was, the negatives that weren't false got him ten months later.

I wonder where exactly he stopped his reading on these pages. Was it where the teenage Karl Ove sneaks home drunk after a debauched New Year's Eve adventure with his mates? His parents look at him but notice nothing. He comments on the past episode: 'No bounds. That was what it was, a feeling of boundlessness.'

Maybe that's what made John reach for a pen and make a note of his symptoms. His own sense of impending bounds, his finiteness.

Or was it the following and hilarious passage – with a nod at Woody Allen or the young Portnoy – where Karl Ove is plagued by worry about the upright direction of his erection and certain that his misshapen dick will prevent him from ever going to bed with anyone.

That, too, might have made John reach for the notepad. Men are men.

I struggle to find the passage I had originally gone to the book in search of, something about meaning and the time of childhood, and how it all vanishes for Karl Ove's father, for adults, into the generality of cares that confound our passage through life. But I keep getting stuck on the dead, the way we conceal them, wrap them up, get them closer to the ground, all funeral parlours being on the ground floor – 'As though we possessed some kind of chthonic instinct, something deep within us that urges us to move death down to the earth whence we came.'

I give up.

When we got home from that brief holiday where John's list was made and stashed in *A Death in the Family*, he gets straight down on the floor with Manny, his playmate. In the first set of pictures and videos that mark our return, they're both down under the table. Manny takes off a sock and stares at his toes with his rapt, intent gaze. 'Toes,' John croons as if they have never been seen before, and carefully extends one from the next while Manny gazes with fascinated curiosity at this world which is ever new.

Then tries to put his sock on his ear. John laughs. He is drunk with it all. I am too. I'm taking the pictures.

I remember now that Baudelaire thought convalescents shared the inspired attentiveness of little ones and artists. In fact, convalescence was a return to childhood. 'The convalescent, like the child, enjoys to the highest degree the faculty of taking a lively interest in things, even the most trivial in appearance,' he writes.

In this house, Manny apart, we are all convalescents. Some of us just take longer over it.

4

THERE IS SOMETHING utterly unique in the relation of grand-parents to their wee ones. We have all the time in the world for Manny while our own runs out. And when I descend into the time of play and goo-goos and high-pitched babble, time vanishes, with my own vanishing time. His, too. My John's.

In the twenty-three months they had of each other, Manny rode on his shoulder, bounced on his chest, took his first steps, became an olive fiend, swam in the sea, kicked waves and sand-castles and leaves, made towers of cups and sent them flying, stared into the mirror and saw something that might have been himself, pointed here, there and everywhere, and learned the basics of language and meaning.

Play, when I reflect on it a year and half after John has gone, is itself already an eternity, a timeless zone, bracketed from the rush and crush of things. It makes time slow and disappear. It removes it from the realm of measurement. It's a perfect accompaniment to mourning where time makes little sense. A sudden memory rushes you towards the Pont des Arts in Paris and you're walking along arm in arm as if everything is present and future and the past itself is different. And you land in Archway in an empty house where the resident ghost is angry and the clock tells you that in three minutes you'll be late for a meeting.

Unlike John, I'm an impatient person – except when I'm writing, which I guess isn't unlike play, but play all by oneself. With Manny, I'm other. I'm neither old nor young, neither wrinkled nor fat nor thin. And if I am, such things are items of curiosity. Most of all, I'm *grand*. Big, not little. I'm a grand-parent – though once he has language, he calls me Nana. With Manny, I can chase shadows for hours, or as many minutes as he wants to before the next game starts. We watch ants and slugs and name the flowers in the garden.

Unlike me, he remembers names. 'Helianthemum' rolls off his tongue, if he's in the mood.

We kick and throw crab apples and balls into basketball hoops or at each other. We make sure not to walk on the cracks in the pavement lest the bears or those eternal dinosaurs come out. Tall tales, rhymes, silly songs about any- and everything accompany our escapades. He listens with rapt attention, join-ing in when prodded.

He recognizes the story voice instantly. He can distinguish it from others. He doesn't like to be in the stories himself, not yet. And he has a fascinating relationship to the art on the walls. He stares, he points and tells me things. The paint-ings are often of his mother and father, though of course the painters didn't know that. He's scared of some of these latter images. They're angry, he tells me. He thinks all the men are his father. One of them is. Not the others. He eyes these images from a distance, and every time we cross in front of one he pauses. I have elaborated and repeated that neither this one, nor this one, nor that is of his father. He doesn't want to believe me. When he has learned to speak more clearly and pauses to check out the largest drawing on the landing, he declares: 'That's *not* my daddy.' Like me, he knows that negatives only hide their positives momentarily.

Reader, he is endlessly fascinating. I adore him. I adore him the way one adores the other when one is in love. I idealize him, and he transforms me into someone other, someone I rarely am, perhaps the best of me. It's pure, untrammelled projection.

All this is magnified by the knowledge that this rapture is inevitably fleeting. He will very soon and inevitably be someone else. If he isn't already he will, any minute now, be far more interested and emotionally vested in a world I have nothing to do with. This is a necessarily unrequited love and all the grander for that.

I am so glad that John had Manny in those last two years of his life.

As for myself, I am so glad that I have had him for a little friend a whole day and night each week throughout the grieving rage of mourning. I suspect it was the madness of this counter-balancing love that helped to lift me out of the claws of the first.

5

PROUST'S *À la recherche du temps perdu* is one of the few great novels I know in which a grandmother figures large. It's not a fairy tale, that domestic form, in which all members of an extended family play vital parts and grand – or god or fairy godmothers, or terrifying old Baba Yagas, float in and out. But *À la recherche,* for all the world-weariness of its aristocrats and demi-mondaines, is also, pivotally, a family novel, a book about childhood. Its narrator, Marcel, holds on to the child in him throughout, inadvertently repeating much of what became part of his make-up in those early scenes in the pastoral world of Combray, where he tossed and turned in bed awaiting the kiss that brought solace and sleep from a mother busy entertaining downstairs.

While Marcel's mother is swathed in a desire that produces anxiety in him, just as he does in her as he turns into a sickly child and adolescent, his grandmother is a figure of pure benevolence. When he's a febrile youth plagued with nerves and difficulty in breathing, she takes him to the seaside – to Balbec (in fact Cabourg) on the Norman coast of France, with its wide, sandy beaches and fresh breezes. Here, from their top-floor adjoining rooms at the Grand Hotel, sky and sea are visible and Proust notes the fluctuations of the day reflected on his walls. Here, too, he meets the dashing young women of the 'little band', '*impitoyables et sensuelles*' – unpitying and sensual, as changeable as the sea – who will mark his rites of passage into manhood. Like Albertine, with whom he will eventually live, the rakish, daring young women, speeding by on their bicycles, are filled with the danger and enticements of the unknown.

Marcel's grandmother stands firmly unmoving and in contrast to them. She is a perpetual reader and citer of the letters of Madame de Sévigné, a witty and astute commentator on the manners and mores of her time. Like Marcel's grandmother, perception is important to that habitué of the French court. It is a faculty that comes to influence Marcel's own writing. Beyond personal desires – whether for meetings with the aristocracy or for complicated foods – Marcel's grandmother imbues him with her taste, her love of beauty and nature. Above all she is a touchstone of the moral. A figure of great kindness, generosity and goodwill, she also understands and accepts Marcel for whatever he is.

> I knew, when I was with my grandmother, that
> however great the misery that was in me, it would
> be received by her with a pity still more vast, that
> everything that was mine, my cares, my wishes,
> would be buttressed, in my grandmother, by a desire
> to preserve and enhance my life that was altogether
> stronger than my own; and my thoughts were

continued and extended in her without undergoing
the slightest deflection, since they passed from my
mind into hers without any change of atmosphere or
of personality.

She is there for him. There, in the middle of the night if
he is feverish, early in the morning if he needs her, pushing
open the shutters to narrate to him the look of the day, the
movement in the street, the small murmurings of everyday life.
In the Proustian world, where relations are rarely simple and
unconflicted, she stands out as a rare solace.

There is, however, one anguished moment between them
during their Balbec stay. After having submitted his impres-
sions of his life that day to her, and she has sieved them, Marcel
blurts out, 'I couldn't live without you.'

His grandmother is troubled. She says to him that he
mustn't speak like that. He must be stronger. 'Otherwise what
would become of you, if I went away on a journey. But I hope
that you would be sensible and quite happy.'

Marcel protests, only then to realize she is speaking of that
ultimate journey. Of death. He's distressed, but to assuage
her, he says, 'You know what a creature of habit I am. For the
first few days after I've been separated from the people I love
best, I'm miserable. But though I go on loving them just as
much, I get used to their absence, my life becomes calm and
smooth. I could stand being parted from them for months, for
years . . .' He doesn't go on. He turns brusquely to stare out of
the window. His grandmother leaves the room.

What he uttered as an excuse to make her happy does indeed come to pass, once the rites of passage into manhood, which she has overseen, are over.

After the holiday in Balbec, Marcel goes off with friends. His grandmother returns to Paris. When she next appears in the book's life, it is as a disembodied voice on the telephone – still, then, a shocking new technology. Her voice is full of sweetness, and a fragility that seems 'on the verge of breaking, of expiring in a pure flow of tears'. This severed voice tears at Marcel's heart: 'This isolation of the voice was like a symbol, an evocation, a direct consequence of another isolation, that of my grandmother, for the first time separated from me.' It is a premonition of her death, and he cries, 'Granny!' longing to kiss her, to return to Paris. 'Granny,' he cries, to her voice, to that 'phantom as impalpable as the one that would perhaps come back to visit me when my grandmother was dead'. 'Speak to me,' he insists to the telephone, but the uncertain line is now disconnected.

Soon after, his grandmother falls ill. With his customary irony and unflinching observation of Marcel's own and others' emotions, Proust sets the scene of her stroke in a public toilet on the Champs-Élysées, outside which Marcel waits for her impatiently, worrying that he will miss his rendezvous with friends. Illness and death are ever an inconvenience in Proust's fashionable world. The witty observations of the medical profession, their conflicting recommendations for a woman who is old and on whom time will take its inevitable toll, whether a little sooner or a little later, add a layer of irony to the responses of friends and acquaintances to the fact of her approaching death. The very gravity and pathos of death act as indicators of fashionable character. When confronted by their friend Swann's announcement of his imminent death, the Duc and Duchesse of Guermantes care more about fetching her red party shoes than attending to Swann's news.

One morning, not long after the grandmother's stroke in the Champs-Élysées, Marcel's mother wakes him to tell him gently, 'My poor child, you have only your papa and mamma to rely on now.' He goes to his grandmother's bedside, kisses her, feels her hands quiver and a long shudder go through her whole body. After a moment, she sits up, opens her eyes, and expires. An hour or two later, after her hair has been combed out, the 'strains and hollows which pain had carved' on her face have vanished.

As in the far-off days when her parents had chosen
for her a bridegroom, she had the features, delicately
traced by purity and submission, the cheeks glowing
with a chaste expectation, with a dream of happiness,
with an innocent gaiety even, which the years had
gradually destroyed. Life in withdrawing from her
had taken with it the disillusionments of life. A smile
seemed to be hovering on my grandmother's lips.
On that funeral couch, death, like a sculptor of the
Middle Ages, had laid her down in the form of a
young girl.

6

I NEVER KNEW any of my grandparents. Only one grandmother remained alive after a world war that had carried away
the others. I have a hazy recollection from somewhere in my
earliest Polish life that may well be of my mother's mother.
It's of a white head floating in a white space far above me.
There are eyes of a pale, strangely glaucous blue, unlidded,
like a bird's. I don't know whether this image has floated into
my mind from a lost photograph long ago, or an experience,
but I have determined that it belongs to my grandmother, ill
in a clinic in Lodz where, according to my parents, she died
soon after I had come with them for a visit. If this image has
lingered in my mind for so many years, it can only be because
the scene it comes from was freighted with emotion, indeed
fear. I was probably almost two. A hunt for records from that
distant post-war where life had not yet taken on ordinary
forms only resulted in a dead end. The civic building where
such records might have been kept burned down well before
I got to it.

When I first read Proust as a graduate student, I was
interested in the grandmother as an ethical force young

Marcel needs somehow to tear away from to launch himself into an adult world of desire. Now I find his depiction of Marcel's relations with his grandmother so poignant it brings tears. It's his recognition that she will do anything for him, yet she must also be left behind, so that he can move into a life away from that whole family aegis: move into his own life, through which she can only echo, like the bells of distant spires.

I'm also now moved by it because it's to do with death, whose presence in my life is more actual than it has ever been before.

I don't think our little Manny, on the cusp of his second birthday, understood anything of John's dying. He hadn't yet mastered the telephone, so though we tried, we don't think he altogether registered the disembodied voice over the sound waves from the hospital. Nor did he then, as far as I can gather, have any sense of time and its passing – a year later he refused to believe he had ever been a baby. Nor can he now recall John's last outing with him. I do.

It was a crisp autumnal day, 30 October 2015, and in Waterlow Park the leaves of the maples and cherry trees were an iridescent red. There is a photograph of Manny held aloft into the embrace of a luminous tree close to the small lake. He is wearing a puffy red jacket and he reaches up into the glow of the branches, leaning back against his grandpa's chest. Only John's dark eyes are visible behind him. But there's a crease in them and we know he's smiling. A few photos along in the sequence, past the feeding of the ducks, he and Manny have trekked through brambles and are propped by the rail of the cemetery. It is through there that John's grave now lies. This was the last walk we all had together.

After he died, Manny never mentioned him, never asked where he was. He couldn't really because he didn't speak much more than a few words. But there was no sign that he noticed his absence. He never said, 'Where's Papa?' which was what he called him. He just accepted that he was gone.

While John was ill or, as they say, in treatment, and I couldn't seem to do much, I wrote some rhyming stories for Manny about his adventures with his grandfather in the lands of 'near and far' and 'now and then'. A talented young artist started to illustrate them and never finished, and I never perfected them. But I can read them to Manny. At times he likes them. And he seems to recognize who that picture of the 'papa' is.

Even though we have all been within them, the minds of children are mysterious. I don't know whether, somewhere within the complexity of his neural and chemical make-up, Manny has a bodily memory of having once had a twin – of being, in that sense, himself already a survivor. Nor do we know what children pick up from the conversations or gestures around them. It's certainly far more than we credit them with.

What I do know is that after John's death Manny became my weekly treat: the burden of anger and madness seemed to dissipate only in his presence. We played. We built Lego towers that toppled or trains that had dogs for drivers. He would lift one of the letters on his letter board from its little slot, then put it back in the right place a few minutes later with no problem; then he would lift it up and, with a mischievous look in his eyes, try to force it back in the wrong way round. And I would exclaim, 'No, it's upside down.' He would do this again and again, then blithely put it back the right way round. Maybe the grin was telling me that the right ways were never as simple as they seemed, even if you knew what they were.

The next day, having spent the night in his cot, he'd go home, and I would return to being a raging woman under the calm façade (or so I hoped) that chaired meetings and panels or talked to friends.

7

MY OWN CHILDREN had a strong attachment to my mother, and my son, briefly, too, to my dad, who died after Josh was already in command of language. My mother, who had been born during one world war and lived through another, brought history into their midst in an anecdotal daily way, giving them a glimpse of strange, remote lands where people inhabited other customs and had been through terrifying ordeals. It's perhaps no surprise that my son, who had the double benefit of her and visiting Italian grandparents, whose memories stretched back to before the First World War, trained as an anthropologist: there were already so many strange tribes at home, with their idiosyncratic dialects, rites and fully displayed superstitions.

Nor was it easy for the children to witness a grandmother, who had been increasingly dotty, succumb to Alzheimer's and cease to recognize the two beings she had doted on above all others. My son made a moving film about her, lost in her nursing-home, cast loose from her mental moorings. Increasingly, in her last years, time had pulled her back into the drama of her war years and away from the present. I suspect part of our daughter's impetus to study history came not only from her dad but from this grandmother, who inhabited it so dramatically, before it vanished from her altogether in her last illness.

The tales families tell or mask tumble through the generations and accrue new meanings. Sometimes these leave conscious traces; at others you see their echo in bodily habits or lilts of the voice. They can be distorted to suit new needs or feed political resentments, but they rarely vanish altogether.

Recently I had the notion of downloading the photos from John's mobile, something I had never thought of doing before. Or perhaps I had dreaded the thought. I found the last photo he had taken of little Manny. It was in the garden on a bright day. Manny is looking down at the leaves scattered here and there on the grass. John's shadow is tall behind and above him – but their heads are on the same plane, as if Manny were once more seated on his shoulder.

The personal past will be a strange, crowded place for my grandchildren, the most photographed generation in history. In place of the single distant unreliable mental image I have of a grandmother, there will be thousands to choose from. It may well be that the images themselves, which I ponder over with such detailed attention, scouring their backgrounds for clues to distant life, will have become meaningless or will vanish with the iCloud they live on. Who knows whether memory, itself now so charged with visual weight, may be transformed in the knowledge that information is so easily stored elsewhere? Loss, too, may well take on a whole new set of meanings. Hauntings will be different – Manny will be able to hear our voices as he grows up, without any need of internalizing them. A new mental configuration for humans suddenly appears very close, though I also imagine that every generation nearing its end may think that a future that won't contain them will be radically different.

The only thing I suspect will stay the same for a little while yet is the fact that we die, and at the other end that we're born, by whatever means a little help from science will render available.

8

TODAY WOULD HAVE BEEN John's birthday, the second since his death. Coming in the dog-days of summer, his birthdays always coincided with essential cricket cup matches or other sporting fixtures. Tension hovered over celebrations. Yet I find photos now of birthday gatherings with the children and friends, and he's always smiling. He looks so happy. Maybe I'm wrong about the strain. Maybe I'm misremembering, shrouding the past in a retrospective pall.

Now that I consider it, the lead-up to the events themselves was what he didn't like to be reminded of. The insistent marking of the passage of a time that inevitably runs out. Some of us like the marking out: the fuss, the toasts, the specialness momentarily stop the rapid rush. For John, the very observance accentuated the speed of passage. We had a similar difference in our relationship to deadlines. The weight of the deadline, the order from above, was so hard for me to bear that I could hear the seconds ticking and had to finish a book or article if possible before it was due, or at least to submit on time. Personally punctual, John was oblivious to deadlines: time was just the time of a match or a time signature in music.

Though it had to start on time, it could always be started again.

Yet he's smiling in those birthday pictures. I shall have to alter my inner perception of his likes and dislikes. Our differences. That alteration may be how the process of re-idealization begins.

It has already begun.

PART OF ME WAS LATE for the content of John's wonderful obituaries. I hadn't anticipated the shock, the anger of grief, the way it stirs you up and chokes you on the worst, disorients, turns you into a raging being, drives you mad. It was why I began on this somewhat humiliating story of mine: I have always believed that if I felt something, others must too, even if such matter is rarely spoken. The widows and widowers I have met, even those of an age where death is usual, look shocked. They're not altogether steady on their feet. Their eyes wander. They occasionally lose their train of thought or talk for just a little too long, or fall silent for no reason in the midst of a conversation. They're agitated, internally preoccupied. What may have been a long bout of a partner's illness has jarred them in unexpected, idiosyncratic ways.

Only now did I feel ready for what I had always thought mourning was meant to be about – a celebration of a good enough life. Not that I have any illusions that the bad stuff will ever be wholly eradicated, but perhaps somehow overlain, the jagged contours less wounding.

Memory is meant to be the faculty by which our identity is constituted. Mine has always felt slippery, which is perhaps why I ended up spending years researching it from lab to litera-ture. It's clear that recollection is prompted and also coloured by whatever it is that sets it off. Much disappears and is re-edited, according to what present emotions need, or need to annihilate about the past. The title of my first novel, *Memory and Desire*, was sparked not only by the extraordinary opening of T. S. Eliot's *The Waste Land* but by what the analyst Wilfred Bion noted: 'Memory is the past tense of desire.'

Childhood is largely an atmosphere in which some key events figure large. It can take on more moment when we're involved with our own children or grandchildren. My own early life is largely unremembered terrain: my parents back then were the kind of immigrants who focused far more emphatic-ally on the future than on the past. Anticipation is a mood I recognize far more readily than nostalgia.

Much of my everyday life as an adult with its necessary habits is a blur. What was I thinking, for instance, on the morning of 10 September 2001? My work diary holds only appointments and I have rarely kept a journal. I might have been writing and then, in any case, I would have been oblivious to my own life: I almost never have memories of writing, which is something of a trance state. Yet, like many others, I remember the next day, 9/11 clearly: that's a collective memory, reinforced by a barrage of images so dramatic that when I first saw the planes, the blazing Twin Towers, after my son had emailed me a mes-sage to turn on the telly, I thought one of his goofy montages of that period had made it to daytime television.

But if I'm me, despite the fact that so many of my days have left little conscious trace, I must also be all the things I've forgotten. That's a relief. I have now forgotten so much that, if I remembered it all, I'd be so heavy, gravity would pull me downwards every time I took a step. Or my head would be as vast as one of those Easter Island monoliths, and I'd topple over. No wonder they don't have legs to propel them.

That's what our unconscious must also be. All those forgettings, forever shifting around, disappearing because we don't want or need them, merging with others, reappearing to make decisions for us we don't know how we arrived at, playing tricks on us or tossing us unwittingly into loves and hates.

9

MANNY SITS AT THE HEAD of our long, rectangular table. He is eating. He sips thick green courgette soup. He munches avocado. He adores red peppers and spinach, relishes pickles and smoked fish. His favourite dessert is mango. He is the child of a foodie generation. My children at his age rarely let anything but chips and apples cross their lips, maybe an occasional chocolate ice cream.

I watch him and my mind wanders. All the dinners I have prepared. All the wine John poured. This table has hosted so much conviviality. So many friends. Writers, artists, filmmakers, campaigners, politicians, analysts, publishers, academics, scientists, journalists, family. I can conjure up visitors who brought into the room an atmosphere of such stately quietude that the space was transformed into a chapel or convent. I can hear voices full of spiky wit or provocation, inflected with a multiplicity of accents. I can taste stories so brilliant in their unfolding that I wish I could conjure every word. There are hoots of laughter and saucy gossip. There are arguments too, passion, heat, debate. Politics, strategy, books, life. The years rush backwards. The smoke of countless cigarettes wafts into the room and out again.

How I wish I had kept a journal. I didn't. And now so much has gone astray. Lost conversations, remembered warmth. I start to write down some names, then give up. There are so many years now, I would have to write a book that contained only names and I would never complete it, never recall it fully.

John stored things for me. Not only on his computer, but in his mind. He remembered differently and different things. I can conjure up places, and through them events and people, grasp a social moment, even unearth a date through the process. He'd remember dates and what was said, though not necessarily by whom. He kept lists of our travels, my CV and his, books. Between us, if the prompts were right, we could conjure up our lives together, conversation with friends and children, arguments, the vitality of discussion, history speeding past.

It makes me think memory isn't altogether a solitary faculty. Perhaps the self isn't either, whatever our conceptions of the individual. We're all made up of others, of our loves, of bits of the times we inhabit, the places we have sniffed and wandered, the exchanges we have had, the books we have read and forgotten. Maybe my parents, my friends, my long-time lovers and companions, my children are as much me as the distressed being pictured on those passports that require an increasing amount of bureaucratic and digital effort to come by. In any case, that passport me never renders an identity that I think resembles me. No wonder border guards look at people so sceptically, distrusting any self they might present outside the one between those embossed covers.

I listen to Manny, who's developing the gift of the gab, though it isn't always comprehensible. His gaze speaks eloquently.

The first years, precisely when all those neural connections are at their most active, are the ones most difficult to situate yourself inside. Before language takes a real grip on mind. My earliest times in Poland are quite gone. Even journeys to the sites where that early me unfolded resulted in no 'Aha' moments that weren't also imaginary.

There are photographs. A beribboned little girl in a knitted white dress with bows in her hair, sitting next to her mother, who holds a children's book. Thanks to modern zoom technology, I can now see this is an English-language primer. I had no idea of that for many decades. There's another image of a similar enough plump toddler, with a beret on her dark hair. She is ensconced in a rather snazzy toy roadster, a version of the kind Agatha Christie characters drive on the telly. Now why, no matter how hard I try, can't I remember the me who's doing the driving, one hand on the wheel, the other on a large bulb of a horn? Or anything about post-war Poland? Not from the inside.

Nor does my memory improve much when I've turned three and four and have language. I've been transmogrified into a little French girl, though still with the hair accoutrements that seem to attend all photographic moments. I'm standing on what looks like the first gallery rung of the Eiffel Tower. I'm not smiling. But I should remember. It's an impressive building. I don't.

There is a trace of a rare smile on my face when, white-stockinged legs folded beneath an aproned skirt topped with a sweater, I'm kneeling beside a large white duck, who doesn't seem to mind being patted. I know, because I've been told, that that's me parked out in the countryside near Paris with a farming family while my immigrant parents tried to create a life in the city. I should remember that duck at least. Nothing comes to me.

Maybe it's the black-and-white of the photos that's at fault. I've been turned into a historical moment. I once found a postcard in a shop in Paris of a little girl standing on a bridge and staring wistfully down the Seine: I was convinced she was me. We were so alike, in the photos at least.

What I remember of Paris in those long-ago days, and I know it's someone who might be me doing the remembering, since no one else could have told me about it, are bodily things. I remember the perfume of apple doughnuts fried in the street and the tart explosion of them in my mouth. I remember stairs that are too steep for my short legs and a slight sense of vertigo and effort as I try to climb and not fall in half-light. I remember a trough-like tub that was cold on the skin if you accidentally leaned on the edge where the water from the steaming kettle didn't reach. The tub was perched on a table or a counter, somewhere high up, too high, and I wanted to climb down to where that bright red armchair magically turned into a bed. Sometimes my parents would go out at night and I was left in that bed in what I latterly discovered was the rue des Archives. I knew I was meant to be a brave girl and not cry, but I wanted to. I didn't, but I wanted to. In their stories, my parents always said I didn't cry, but maybe I did. They wouldn't know. They weren't there. Maybe I wasn't brave.

Sniff. Taste. Up. Down. Scared. Red. Bed. Brave. What's left of my earliest childhood. More or less.

John remembered far more than I did of his childhood, most of which had taken place within a ten-mile London radius. The story he liked most to tell was of their second-year teacher asking the boys who among them had never told a lie. John's hand shot up. Who knows whether that embarrassing moment contributed to him writing a book called *Truth Games*?

10

It is 17 march 2016. John has been gone for exactly four months. I'm taking the tube to West London. Today is another D-day. Today is the day a second baby is due. A baby brother for Manny.

Manny is excited about the baby, or so we think. He is a modern urban child and, so far as a toddler of two and a bit can understand things, he understands that there is a baby in his mother's capacious tummy. For months, he has been crawling up on the sofa to put his ear to the baby's heartbeat, to stroke and hug, and has been taking part in the general anticipation of arrival. It is clear from his behaviour that his delicious mummy is even yummier and cuddlier with this big tummy that is also his.

I'm on duty for however long the birth takes. Manny and I get up to our usual high jinks, though now at his end of town. We chase pigeons on the track along the river, toot-toot the train in the playground, check out the progress of the daffodils. We read books and tell stories. Some of these have little brothers in them who always adore their big brothers.

Once his ragged, unsleeping parents have gone off to the

hospital the next morning, I keep an ear out for the phone and check my messages with rare regularity. I know Manny is aware of that. Parental worries ever translate themselves to children, and during the night that they're away, he's unusually fretful and keeps asking for his mum and dad. But he's bright enough the next day.

His parents arrive home very late that afternoon. It's already growing dark. They're carrying his little brother. Manny looks at his parents, who are making introductions in voices of fatigued excitement. Then he looks at the baby. After a moment of attempted hellos, a shattering howl of despair comes out of him. It's a prolonged, agonized moan. I have never heard anything like it from him before. Or, indeed, from anyone. I can only characterize it as existential – as if his very being were under attack. He is inconsolable.

He tries, with the promise of chips and the antics of his dad, to come back to himself – but that self doesn't seem to be at home. He looks as if he's been knocked off his perch. Literally. From one moment to the next. From the moment of anticipation to the moment of arrival. He looks as if someone has hit him. He's dazed, distraught. He sobs.

The change has come in a single overwhelming instant. There's now this tiny creature attached to his mother's breast, who wasn't there when she left. He hadn't expected that, it's clear. Hadn't expected it at all.

Whatever words may have conveyed to him, whatever picture books he looked at, they didn't create the tangible presence of another, another who has displaced him. Nor will his mother, in discomfort as she now is, let him snuggle into her tum with her usual alacrity. Her body was his. She was his. Whatever rights his father might have had, Manny's came first. Now there's this other creature attached to her whom they call his brother, but who has absolutely nothing to do with him. Worse, this creature called a baby has priority with her. He's always busy with her yucky milk – as they now tell him it's called to dissuade him from wanting it. Big boys don't. And he's a big boy. So he doesn't want it. But neither does he want his brother. And he isn't really a very big boy. He's not big at all. He's little, but he can't climb up on his mummy. He's angry and he looks lost and he won't accept consolation from anyone who isn't his mum. And not even, altogether, from her. No matter how much he wants her. This is betrayal of the first order.

As the days and weeks and months go by, I watch him trying to accommodate himself to his loss of priority, this betrayal of trust. I start humming 'Space Oddity' again. I think to myself, he has lost his innocence. He has fallen from grace. He is being torn apart by conflicting emotions he can neither understand nor control. He is racked by jealousy. And his nearest and dearest have perpetrated this suffering on him.

On top of it all, they sometimes tell him he must love this new creature who is attached to his mother. Love, how can he love? He doesn't want it to be today, or tomorrow, or the next day and the next, while the baby is still here. Love his brother, when all this, this incomprehensible blight on his days, is his brother's fault. What do they mean by love?

Poor little Manny, all of two and a quarter and he's miserably trapped in an utterly ordinary event. An everyday madness takes over this small embattled boy.

11

I DO NOT EXAGGERATE Manny's inner turmoil. When I see him over the coming months, his impish fun in the world is hard to unearth. He is uninterested in food and games, or at least he can only be distracted for a short time. His curiosity has ebbed. His ability to concentrate, to be attentive, which was so great before, has gone too. He is angry, perhaps even angrier than me during those months of grieving, but his emotions are equally or more inchoate. His brother's name comes up in the middle of conversations for no reason. He chants a naptime mantra under his breath. 'Isaiah, Isaiah, Isaiah,' he repeats, his tiny fist clenching the blanket, until he falls asleep. Like an obsessed lover, the name is on his lips when he wakes up. Little brother is there all the time, even when he isn't. He can't be got rid of. He seems to blot out everything else in Manny's life.

Sibling jealousies are well known. Augustine in *The Confessions*, writes,

> I have myself seen jealousy in a baby and know
> what it means. He was not old enough to talk, but,

ıenever he saw his foster brother at the breast, he would grow pale with envy . . . Such faults are not small or unimportant, but we are tender-hearted and bear with them because we know that the child will grow out of them. It is clear that they are not mere peccadilloes, because the same faults are intolerable in older persons.

Freud notes how the older child feels

dethroned, despoiled, prejudiced in its rights; it casts a jealous hatred upon the new baby and develops a grievance against the faithless mother which often finds expression in a disagreeable change in its behaviour. It becomes 'naughty', perhaps irritable and disobedient and goes back on the advances it has made towards controlling its excretions . . . A child's demands for love are immoderate, they make exclusive claims and tolerate no sharing.

Manny's parents are wonderful with him, but he suffers his predicament nonetheless. He begins to hide things. He isn't as companionable at nursery. He hits someone. He's not interested in learning things. He has secrets. They're very open, but they're also secret. He no longer seems to know how to hide in hide-and-seek games and always just wants to be found. Maybe hiding is too scary. Maybe nobody will want to find him again.

The images on my stairs grow scarier, too. Particularly a large drawing of a grizzled, moustached, bare-chested and bespectacled man reading a newspaper in a striped deckchair on a beach. He's sitting next to a woman, but Manny never notices the woman. It's the man he insists is his dad he's intent on. All this drawn man shares with his father is gender, but he's terrified of him. In Manny's eyes, no matter how much I explain, this remains one very angry dad-man, as furious as Manny was when his brother was brought home. I have to hold his hand and protect him to go past the drawing. The nearby self-portrait his father sketched at school, which is a good likeness, also frightens him, but not so horribly as the beach man who seems to stand in for all paternity – *Le nom du père*, the French would say, a culture that's been to collective school with the psychoanalyst Jacques Lacan.

I ask Manny whether his dad shouts at him a lot. No, he says, though I know he does on occasion. His fantasy dad is palpably far scarier than his real dad. It's probably because he's feeling guilty and is worried about punishment – castration anxiety, Freud might have said, which only means fearing you'll be cut down to teeny size from the omnipotent feeling your mum first gave you when she answered all your cries and you adored each other. Punishment in Manny's internalized world seems to be in the offing at every moment: loving his little brother, demanded and expected as it is and sometimes even felt, is proving so difficult. Isn't his just being there punishment enough? His own uncontrollable desires to hurt are far more murderous, I suspect, than what he acts out, however surreptitiously. They're not approved, even by himself. And he's already feeling guilty, even before he's done very much. But he's so young, he can't really express his inner anguish or tell us what kinds of thoughts and fantasies run through his mind.

Whenever I see the boys together, Manny has an arm round his brother, as if he wants to hug him, but the hug inadvertently turns into a stranglehold. It's the same with a pat that somehow turns into a pinch, or a kiss that mutates into a painful squeeze. Yet he can't keep his arms off the baby. He has to cuddle until Isaiah cries or screams. Undoubtedly, as a result of all this, Isaiah has developed an ear-piercing alert signal. We can't keep our eyes off them for an instant.

That grizzled, spectacled man at the top of the stairs is watching, too, even when Manny's real dad or his real brother isn't in the room.

This isn't all. Whatever Manny's doing, whether it's running about with the balls or the sticks he has now developed a liking for, or resting, he can't rid himself of his obsession with Isaiah. We're having a walk and chasing our shadows: he suddenly shouts, 'Isaiah,' and stamps on the ground. He bites into an apple, and Isaiah turns up. We're singing songs he knows perfectly well, and he interpolates them with his brother's name.

One, two, buckle my Isaiah . . .

The grand old Duke of Isaiah . . .

And so on.

It begins to be tedious, as the obsessions of another person inevitably are. The Isaiah tic endears him to no one. I think he knows, but there is nothing he can do. He just somehow has to get through and we have to help and hold him along the way. Punishment will do little except make us feel better, and only for a very short time. But the exclamation 'No!' becomes the most often used in my vocabulary.

Manny starts wanting to dress up all the time. He becomes a superhero, complete with cape. It's good to be big and strong. It's super to be in control of the uncontrollable. First, Spiderman who can stick to anything (I have a suspicion he'd really like to stick to Mummy), is his favourite. Then Superman, then Batman. But any masked being will do. He's even happy wearing the Bottom donkey mask I buy him. He races around happily, makes grand entrances at gatherings. Anything is far better than being himself. In fact, I suspect he feels more himself, far freer, when he masquerades than as that poor torn creature who is driven to repeat 'Isaiah' all the time and be good to him. Superheroes are big, strong and powerful. They're not just tiny boys who are enjoined to be big boys and behave like big brothers.

He also throws the occasional wobbly – a whopper of a tantrum. He's so angry. It's a frustration rooted not only in his brother's very existence, but because he can't have his own way, even though he's meant to be the big brother. All parents will be familiar with this whether there are siblings or not. The child, often tired and frazzled, takes a tiny restriction – say on his wish to jump from a height, or an emphatic 'no' to watching another cartoon – as a challenge to his (momentary) omnipotence.

In Manny's case, the very independence everyone has been encouraging is frustrated. The explosion of anger is triggered by emotions no different from what we see in adults, whether at home, at work or lately, too often, in the political sphere. The tantrum is the purest manifestation of rage against a challenged omnipotence, against the recognition that we are dependent on others, whether for our very lives or for the functioning of society and the nation. We are not fully in control. It's better to learn that in the nursery than turn into a leader with nuclear weapons and not only Lego to play with.

In her *Memoirs of a Dutiful Daughter*, Simone de Beauvoir has a telling passage on her own remembered tantrums, her flailing arms and legs, the sickening void she would plunge into when her desires were curtailed by adult prohibition.

> My convulsions and the tears that blinded me served
> to shatter the restraints of time and space, destroying
> at once the object of my desire and the obstacles
> separating me from it. I was engulfed in the rising
> dark of my own helplessness; nothing was left but
> my naked self that exploded in prolonged howls and
> screams.

Early childhood is a time of extremes, including extreme helplessness.

One Monday when Manny has stayed the night – he's in the midst of that arduous, humiliating business of toilet training now as well – I wake up at my usual far too early morning hour and lie there in a reverie. Suddenly I hear an odd sound and I remember that Manny is with me. I always wake well before him, but there is definitely something amiss today that is neither a noise-filled dream nor a ghost playing havoc. I open the door and follow the sound. It isn't coming from Manny's room: the bars are up on the cot, but it's empty. I chase it down the stairs.

Lying in a heap on the mat by the front door is a sobbing very wet and cold bundle. My heart breaks.

'I thought you'd gone, Nana. Everyone's gone.' He weeps. 'I thought you'd left me.'

He seems to feel he's been bad and the bad encompasses a multitude of sins – his wetness, his worries about his brother, his demands, which can turn into tantrums, his littleness, which is also meant to be big and reasonable. Poor little big man.

Do I feel Manny's plight so strongly because his grief echoes my own? Am I reading too much into it all, projecting? His father is partly convinced of it. Maybe I am. And yet . . . and yet . . .

12

ALL THIS IS NEW TO ME. My own children were ten years apart, and what sibling jealousy there was manifested itself quite differently. I can see that, however much his parents adore Manny and want to give him equal attention, as long as his baby brother is attached to his mother's breast and body, and wholly dependent, Manny feels left out, abandoned. The grown-ups have cast him off in favour of his brother. When I mention his disappearance from his bed to his parents, they tell me he has been doing it at home, too, looking for everyone, not finding them, and sobbing.

FOR MONTHS I have been trying a ploy with the boys to counterbalance their home life: when they all come to see me together, I welcome Manny effusively but pay scant attention to his brother. It's not quite denying Isaiah's existence, but it's making sure big brother is noticed first. I don't quite know how Manny is taking this, but once Isaiah becomes more of a person, perhaps about ten months old and has started at nursery alongside his brother, Manny turns to me at the doorstep one day and very firmly, as if he were teaching me the need for good manners, says, 'You forgot to say hello to Isaiah.'

He is slowly becoming his younger brother's keeper. Nursery helps with this. So does Peppa Pig and her little brother George, I imagine: once he starts he can't stop watching the interplay between the two piglet siblings, who in good anthropomorphic fashion represent a contemporary enlightened family, complete with a newish-man dad and a mum who is better at everything. Under the influence of both culture and home, Manny's obsession has abated somewhat. He's still muttering, 'Isaiah,' under his breath, though not quite so much.

One day, after he's told off yet again for trying to all-but-strangle his brother in a neck lock, he explains to his mum, very seriously, 'Mummy, one arm loves Isaiah, but the other one doesn't.'

Oh my, I think, the madness is definitely on the wane. Little Manny has grasped something very difficult. He has given voice to ambivalence, 'fessed up to his own. He hasn't denied those excruciating negative feelings or only acted them out. Nor has he put all the bad into one particular picture or person, as so many deniers can. Manny's own hands, his own intentions, go two ways at once. He has put words to his conflict. Not all that many adults manage it.

There is so much intelligence in this that I want to hug him with all my arms, the good and the bad. Both of which are having their own difficulties.

Soon after this, his mother gives me an account of a splendid after-nursery conversation. The staff had told her that

Manny had said he 'loved' Isaiah, but he only 'liked' Mummy and Daddy.

She asked him, 'Why don't you love Mummy and Daddy?'

'Do you love me?' little-big Manny queried.

'Yes, of course I love you.'

'Well then, Mummy, I love you too,' he declared. Then, moving on to a more philosophical plane, he asked, 'But, Mummy, what *is* love?'

She parried, 'What do you think it is?'

His response apparently flabbergasted everyone within earshot.

'Mummy, is love trials of passion?'

I should point out that Manny, who has long been able to recognize some words, can recognize the name Appignanesi, which is also his. On my study shelves, there are a great many books and he's particularly fascinated by the ones that have his/my name on them. One of these is called *Trials of Passion*, and he has taken to reading this title wherever he sees it. It obviously appeals to him in some mysterious way. Maybe I once said something to him about it. So his comment to his mum was not altogether out of the blue. But the conjunction was wise – wiser than he can know.

Manny's own trials of passion go on for some time – indeed they may well go on throughout his life in reworked forms.

He's curious again, perplexed by things, the way all children are, and observes far more than we think. He's heard the word 'love' a lot – it accompanies cuddles and food and what he's supposed to feel towards various people, which includes anger and hate. No matter how much he wants her, now that his mum has betrayed him, he's not always too sure about her. He wants her too much so sometimes he just avoids her. That's love, too. He's much more often prepared to make do with his dad, who, when he doesn't get angrily exasperated, is really tops at games. They can be boys together and he can propitiate some of those fears of punishment by identifying with him. Sometimes, when he issues an order to me, he sounds just like his dad.

One day he tells his mum very seriously that he has been playing 'mummies and daddies' with two of his school friends, Cataleya and Sophia. 'I was the daddy,' he tells her, and when she asks, 'Who was the mummy?' he declares emphatically, 'Nobody! I was the daddy and Cataleya and Sophia were babies!'

Manny is becoming something of a humorist, as well as living up a little too adequately to his name.

He's coping with his predicament.

13

TODAY THERE ARE more birds in the garden than I've ever seen. Tits with pale lime tums beneath grey cloaks and rings like velvet round their necks; slender robins with elegant breasts, small birds I don't recognize, dozens of them, all swooping from oak to rose to lilac to Judas and back again in a bright flutter and chirping in a stirring cacophony. Why have they all come today? Is it the fresh bright light? Do they like the butterflies? Have we hatched a new species of aphid? Are the neighbourhood cats all away for the weekend? Are they refugees from a war zone?

One of the things that's changed markedly these last months, and is part of the backdrop of growing old, is that all the things I never had time to focus on before have become subjects of pleasure and thrilling spectacle. A shift of light, the flash of a bird's wing, pearl drops of rain on a rose, the ever-changing spectacle of the garden.

All these daily wonders make me miss John. There is no one to share mundane delights with now. These are what shore you up for the travails of the domestic sphere and beyond. The more decades I experience, the more I see daily repetitions and variations on the most ancient dramas in our culture: Antigone in the nursing-home leading her aged, repentant father round the grounds, quarrelling with the family over burial sites after her two brothers have led opposing armies in a civil war; children suffering as a formidable Clytemnestra or raging Medea take revenge on uncaring husbands; a youthful Electra and Orestes plotting against an unfaithful mother; a teenage Telemachus yearning for his father and doing battle with unsuitable suitors as Penelope waits not all that patiently for the return of her wily Odysseus; Jocasta transgressing generational divides and falling unwittingly for her own heroic son, who has pushed away her husband. Such dramas of family life are all around us with their everyday madness. Happily, most of us manage to contain, mute or repress such excessive passions, leaving them behind in childhood and only very occasionally re-enacting their frenzy when they rumble within us.

My John was one of three brothers, each following the other at about four-year intervals. The middle one, John snapped at his older brother's heels and simultaneously learned how to rebel against fraternal edicts. Soon enough, he would have to lay down his own and master the uneasy fraternal art of being tough and tender by turn to a younger sibling. I've often wished I could have been a fly on the wall as their early childhoods unfolded.

This is especially true as I watch Manny and Isaiah at play, the dramatic rivalry over toys, attention and affection. I have long been wondering just how Isaiah will internalize and adapt to his brother's antics, all that pinching and painful squeezing he suffers, those tantrums and the ensuing parental discipline.

Sometimes when his shrill cry and call for help comes, I'm cast back into the younger sister I was. I also think a lot about John wedged between two brothers, alternately little and big in a very different way.

A few months after John's death, his older brother, David, told me a story from their childhoods. It dated from a time when they were the only two brothers. John must have been three or so, Manny's age. The boys' mother had the older child look after the younger. The two of them often went to the local park, where David would be meeting friends for a game of rounders or football. Having a little brother in tow was shaming so David would regularly hide John in the bushes that surrounded the play area. The three-year-old was under strict orders not to emerge or cry until David returned to fetch him. Making his little brother disappear was the best thing David could do, and it's easy to suspect it was also the fulfilment of a daily wish.

Little John did as he was told. I imagine him, as David conjures him, watching the game avidly through the shrubbery, envying the older boys, being excited by their shrieks and activity, but containing his own, refusing tears. In the way that children do, I expect he also got a certain excited pleasure out of his self-mastery and the secrecy of his presence at the game. Their mother never knew: neither boy revealed how things played out between them. Keeping secrets is one of the ways children assert independence from parents, who claim to see and know everything. There is power in it.

Simone de Beauvoir describes her own sense of liberation when she realized her strict mother couldn't see everything she claimed to be able to see, including her early sexual satisfactions. The disaffection from a purportedly all-seeing God came just a little later.

Children can be valiant as well as secretive creatures. The wonder is that they mostly get through these early trials and passions, even if they inevitably leave the marks and scars we call character, and shape the ways they live and love.

14

ENGAGING WITH THE passions of the nursery, with more time at my disposal than I've ever had before in my working life, sparks dreams of my own childhood. Like John, like Isaiah, I had an older brother. Given the wartime ghosts who peopled my early years, and the company of fraught immigrant parents, I never gave too much thought to my brother and the impact he must have had on me. But perhaps that small boy, who towers over me in family photos, is a crucial element in the puzzle that the self perennially is.

The pictures reveal that my brother Stan has a vagrant hand, much like Manny's. It's always pressing down and digging into my shoulder, as if to urge me into the ground – where death lurks and bodies lie supine.

There is something about the way baby Isaiah deals with Manny's onslaught that triggers a bodily memory in me. The littlest one has a habit of bending away from his brother's aggressive hand in a particular fashion. He recoils or stiffens in anticipation of the pinch before it has actually come. Sometimes he's passive, relaxing into the pain. At other times, he screams. The world is not a thoroughly friendly place. It can't altogether be trusted. But when he cries for Mummy, she does come instantly: she cuddles him and scolds the aggressor – as it should be. When he's with her, at least, he's safe.

As the months go by, I suspect Isaiah learns to howl at the merest sign of threat, and even when he just fancies a cry or call: he's sensitive to the menace, has internalized an awareness of it, accommodated it. And he can make use of the threat, as well as of the actual pinch. The cries bring immediate attention from the biggest ones. As a result he's largely a placid, sunny sort of chap. On the surface. In his own way, he's also very determined. He's learning to rebel against his brother. To nab his toys. I sometimes think I can hear him wondering how much he can get away with. But maybe I'm just identifying.

I was the baby. My brother was born just before the war. I arrived six and a half years and an eternity of damaging experience later – not all that long after the war's nominal end, though for my parents its aftermath, both historical and emotional, took years to unfurl. My arrival was the sign of a new beginning for them and, soon enough, a move to another country.

What separates me from my brother is his childhood experience of a murderous history, the constant menace accompanied by perpetual excitement, a visceral need for lies and subterfuge, an Oedipal closeness to his mother, who could disappear at any time. All this was exacerbated by his father's absence or pretence of absence during the years that husband and wife couldn't openly live together as a couple. I have narrated this elsewhere.

The rest of his story is one of the everyday domestic wild, savage in its own more familiar ways.

I was the lucky one, the ordinary enough one, the one who grew into consciousness amid the ducks of rural France, the never-changing Paris streets, then settled in peaceful, orderly Canada. I wasn't the one who had had to change her name at regular intervals, disown her father, live with persecuting men in uniform, guns, bombs, and agonized parental fear. From the vantage-point of adulthood, I understand my brother better.

Back then, he was my very own and utterly unpredictable SS officer. I could rarely discern what would put him into a rage, what might bring lashings. So every time the fraternal hand pressed into my shoulder, I cowered, tried to escape, yelped, or put on the unsmiling, beleaguered face I see in photographs where he stands by my side with a military bearing he might well have picked up from the Gestapo. It's not that he didn't love me. It's that humiliating or punishing the smaller sibling, who takes Mummy away, can be a distinct site of sadistic pleasure.

I think I learned the value of obedience back then – at least an outward compliance. Increasingly, I suspect, it was accompanied by an inner distancing, an inward migration or rebellion.

Remember, I was a girl. Compliance was rewarded.

It may be that one of my clearest early memories finds its context here.

I must have been around six or seven. I'm sitting on a wooden floor, my legs tucked under and behind me in a position that is now intensely uncomfortable. It's quite cold and my dress is scratchy.

I'm thinking that I'm glad to be a girl. It feels like a revelation. I'm happy. Girls don't have to be soldiers. This is the reason I give myself. They don't have to go to war. I feel relieved and privileged.

I've always liked this memory. Not only because it's my first recollection of reflecting on myself through the prism of gender. I like the fact that I manifest this early pride in womanhood.

I don't know what sparked the thought. There seemed to be other, more important, demarcations than gender in my family. There was big. My brother, of course. And small. Me. In school, we were ranked and often lined up according to size, not gender. At home, both my parents were bigger than either of us: authority and thus power came in two genders.

Then there was the difference between the very cold outdoors and the warm interior, particularly warm if you were tucked under a satiny duvet. There was rich, those people who lived on the mountain, and poor – us, though not for long, my parents hoped. There was smart and stupid. It was very important to be the first, which involved reading. Then there was Jewish and not Jewish. The second -ish didn't like the first. My parents had been both and that was somehow mixed up with war.

But the happy fact was that I wouldn't have to be a soldier, even if I got as big as my brother or as rich as the people on the mountain. I was a girl. That seemed to be the only unalterable distinction among all those shifting ones.

Now, with my two oft-warring grandsons in the frame, I wonder whether my early satisfactions in girlhood were prompted by the taunting of an older brother marauding round the house. Am I glad to be a girl because I'm glad not to be my persecuting brother? Is this a dawning moral sense? Or is my insistence on pleasure in my gender hiding the opposite thought? I might well have preferred to be a boy, but rebelling insistently against my brother was essential to survival, marking myself out, finding reasons with which to refute his views and presence.

I add this caveat because it comes to me that, despite this clear memory of my gladness and relief, I always identified with, first, the boys and then the men in the books I read as a child and later as an adolescent. I think I even preferred Mellors to Lady Chatterley when I first secretly devoured the book as a young teenager at the time of the trial, though that might have been an authorial effect – Lawrence patently preferred him, too.

On the other hand, it's clear that in the imagination we can take on any gender. Male authors have imagined splendid female characters, from Moll Flanders to Isabel Archer, and women imagined men, from Darcy to Daniel Deronda, or Marilynne Robinson's Reverend John Ames. Freud theorized a fundamental psychic bisexuality for humans – a sharing of both masculine and feminine attributes in lesser or greater degree.

That seems about right to me. I suspect when you're an immigrant neither bodies nor nations bear the promise of a singular and forever predestined home.

If my dates for my memory of feeling pleased with being a girl are in any way accurate, it must have taken place at the time of the Korean War or just after. Soldiers were much in the news. This in turn would have spurred family arguments, my father ever angry and belligerent beneath his calm surface, my mother scathing about the stupidity of politicians.

What I'm glad about, perhaps, is that I've discovered a good reason not to envy my big brother, even though he's freer and bigger than me, and it's clear that my mother likes him best. But I now know that I don't have to get into fights, or be as pugilistic as he is, particularly a little later when he takes up boxing. I don't think I envy his penis. I've seen it and it doesn't look all that much, and contains far less scary power than his size: he is getting bigger than my dad.

15

ACCORDING TO FAMILY LORE, my brother had tried to suffo-
cate me when I was still in the cradle. He put a pillow over my
head and pressed. My mother arrived in the nick of time. Later,
having been chased round the house by what I remember as
threats, raised fists, and the kind of rampant anger that still
terrifies me, I used to spend many hours locked in the toilet,
evading the harsh discipline of his authority. I'd ring my working mother covertly, relaying a frantic message, then dash off to
hide. Or hide first, wait for quiet – signalling that my brother
might have gone out, or into the basement where he had his
lair – and then dash out to the telephone and hope against
hope that the party line wasn't being used by those invisible
sharers.

When my parents got home, usually late, I'd whimper and
complain. They'd comfort me and tell my brother off. He called
me a mewling snitch, or something similar. Only when he was
away at school and then university did I begin to breathe freely.
With him at home, I always felt like the outsider in the family,
the intruder who'd arrived late, who didn't altogether belong
in the threesome who shared that heavy, significant past. I left

home as soon as I could, at eighteen, and didn't look back – though, of course, in the way of things, home followed me, and the family remained close enough.

Yet as I write these words, I wonder whether, after all, I did envy my brother – his strength, his noise, his apparent self-certainty, his freedoms. I must have a little.

If you ask my brother about all this, the cards were stacked firmly against him towards the little pest who was everyone's favourite, the one who was always paraded about with her tutus and ribbons and who got away with murder.

Later, during the intense years of puberty and early teens, he'd scoff at my looks, call me 'Big Nose', monitor my boy-friends and tear them apart, not physically, though there were ever threats of that, too. By then I'd learned to rebel more overtly, which is just as well because I don't at all approve of the cowering, tattling creature I was. When I was small, I was scared, lonely too, with all the changing of schools and lan-guages, the anxious waiting for parents to come home from work. One of the things that it's so easy to lose track of as an adult is how very much size matters for children – as Alice knew so well in her Wonderland. My brother was much bigger.

I may have been more terrified at first of my brother's phys-ical lashings, but it was his envy and the damage it could do me that were scariest. I could feel it as a palpable presence between us – a thorny briar that had to be negotiated at every turn or you'd be torn apart. Each of his early taunts and insults stayed with me for much of my life. I long thought I was ungainly, ugly, big-nosed, stupid, and so it went on.

My mother didn't or couldn't altogether help: she'd repeat

at any of his wrongs, 'He's always just been jealous of you.' (She used the word 'jealous', since in French '*envie*' also contains the word for 'desire' or 'wish' or 'long for'. Only when it's a question of sin does '*envie*' translate easily into 'envy'.) And then she'd boast of my achievements to him, as if that would make him envy me the less. It didn't. All I wanted to do was disappear. Which I did, first into books, which could dash off and hide with me in the toilet, and later to another place in another country.

I have been terrified of what I can now designate as envy ever after. That terrible evil eye, which threatens bad luck and despoliation. It explains what I always thought was the surprising coincidence that I repeatedly came second in classes. Never first and rarely third. Why was it that my closest friends invariably came first, as if secondariness was in my nature and that pleased me? I didn't like winning; I didn't like being singled out. Until late in life I far preferred being deputy to being head. I liked friends whom I considered far prettier or better disposed or more talented or more something than me. It wasn't just that at various points I might not have been good enough for first place. Or that I was a traditional woman, secondary by social nature. I really do think the fear of being envied, of being despoiled by all those other potential brothers in the world, played its part in the pattern. And being with someone better than you served as some protection from the malicious gleam of the envious eye. I liked disappearing.

'The past' – as my good friend Adam has said, with one of his inimitable Phillipsian turns of phrase – 'influences everything and dictates nothing.'

The best thing about getting old may be that no one envies you. For that reason alone, it is in certain respects a calming and pleasant time.

16

ST AUGUSTINE's envious child looking upon his half-brother at the breast does not want the mother's milk, which he has in any case outgrown. What he wants is his brother's place in their mother's life. And if he can't have that, he'll identify with his brother and demand to be treated with absolute equality. That, too, is impossible since his brother is just more help-less than he is and the elder doesn't necessarily want the baby's helplessness. So the envy becomes contaminated with the wish to spoil whatever it is his brother is getting and, if necessary, him and their mother in the process – even if it means in the end spoiling it for himself as well. That way, at least, everyone is equal.

In one of my very favourite of his essays, John Forrester (the one I call my John) explored the workings of envy in the judgement of Solomon. He showed how the bereaved mother's claim for half a baby, a baby split in half, follows the logic of envy. Deprived of her own child, the bereaved woman wants her friend's living child. If she can't have that, justice will mean that a half-child will do – in other words, neither of them will have a living baby.

The same essay examines Freud's thinking on the 'herd instinct'. Freud looks to the nursery for the origin of later social formations. The group is psychologically constituted as a reaction to life in the nursery: 'the initial envy with which the elder child receives the younger one' is where social feeling comes into being. The elder child

> would certainly like to put his successor jealously
> aside, to keep it away from the parents, and to rob it
> of all its privileges, but in the face of the fact that this
> younger child (like all that come later) is loved by the
> parents as much as he himself is, and in consequence
> of the impossibility of his maintaining his hostile
> attitude without damaging himself, he is forced into
> identifying himself with the other children . . . The
> first demand made by this reaction-formation is for
> justice, for equal treatment for all.

I'm put in mind of David's story about his and John's childhood, and how neither John nor he had ever told their mother about their playground antics and the ritual of John's sequestration in the shrubbery. John might already have identified a part of himself with his older sibling. There is power in being two or eventually three, a band of brothers – a grouping against what my daughter used to call the 'parental unit', designating us by that name either singly or together.

Life in the classroom reinforces the pattern of the group. If you can't be teacher's favourite, no one else should be favourite either. And so group bonds come into being: 'Social justice means that we deny ourselves many things so that others may have to do without them as well.'

This may help to explain why the politics of *ressentiment* or envy, prime movers towards greater equality and justice in many historical moments, so rarely altogether achieve what the envious ostensibly want – though through the struggle they may attain a sense of their own virtue. Think of that great and virtuous revolutionary Robespierre, champion of the poor and of the colonies, advocate for the downtrodden and for the abolition of slavery. To err on the side of reduction here in order to underline a point, Robespierre was himself an eldest child and conceived on the wrong side of marriage vows. He grew to power with his Committee of Public Safety and unleashed the Terror, guillotining king and queen, the aristocracy and his one-time comrades-become-opponents, only to end under the blade himself.

The British referendum on the EU, like the Trump election, could well be characterized in terms of populist *ressentiment* – an equalizing move by the have-nots against the haves, however the haves are envisaged: those with relative wealth, better education, more access to cosmopolitan goods, or simply those immigrants with greater access to welfare services, who also get more attention from the vocal (as opposed to the really rich) parts of the elite. Some of this equalizing is emphatically necessary. I share the angry wish for it. But the outcome of this particular electoral decision may well be that life in the first instance will get worse, be despoiled, for everyone.

I have long loved the teasing maxims of one of the earliest psychologists, that wily old aristocrat La Rochefoucauld, who watched the world with an unflinching eye. One in particular used to perplex me: 'Our envy always lasts longer than the happiness of those we envy.' A modern gloss on it might be 'Our desire is always in excess of our satisfaction.'

The savage life of the nursery has shed a little more light on this all-too-human conundrum for me.

CODA

I think we dream so we don't have to be apart for so long. If we're in each other's dreams, we can be together all the time.

A. A. MILNE, *Winnie-the-Pooh*

LAST NIGHT I HAD A DREAM from which I woke in a state that I can only call happy. Or do I mean peaceful? It has been so long since I have been at peace that I hardly recognize the atmosphere of that state. Let's just say that in the dream, I know I was happy.

John and I are together in a very pretty flat. I don't know it, though it's oddly familiar. The colours, the deep orange stripes and shapes on the carpet atop a golden floor, the pictures, the bright sofa, the light pouring in through the many windows, the interesting lateral spaces make it something like a house built by Frank Lloyd Wright, with one level visible from another to make a wide open expanse.

We're travelling to Paris later that day. The air between us is electric with interest and anticipation. I have to go to the dentist first, but before I leave we kiss. It tastes fresh and flirtatious. We're playful with one another, and as I say good-bye, he picks up a scatter cushion and throws it in my direction. I catch it with a laugh and see it has a *Time* magazine cover printed on it: it shares a cartoon image from one of his own books, but the important thing is, I know, and he says it, 'I'm giving you time.'

I look at him and smile. I realize we're both young. We have so much time.

I go out to find myself on a whitewashed street, somewhere between Notting Hill and Asolo in the Veneto. There are little shops along the way and I think, I'll buy us some things for a treat of a lunch. I give the Vietnamese a miss and decide on the small Italian deli, with its smooth, rounded haunch of ham hanging in the window. Behind the counter there's a queue, and when I get to the front, for some reason I recognize the curly-headed young man and attractive woman behind it and know his name.

'Marco,' I say, and am about to ask him for some slices of prosciutto and salami, when an old, wrinkled woman edges me aside. I decide I had better let her go first.

I wake up.

I'm happy.

I don't quite know why I'm happy. Except that John is young and we're together and he clearly likes me and wants to give me time to enjoy the beauties around us. But I must also be the old woman who pushes me aside. I don't know who Marco is, unless he's a version of my curly-headed son, and the lovely woman beside him is our daughter, both of whom have given me so much of the bounties of life.

I think this is a dream of reconciliation. And what else can one want from the end of a life or a book like this, except a reconciliation – with one's dead, one's living and oneself.

I HAVE TAKEN A LONG JOURNEY. I began with the shock of death and the subliminal ghost-ridden madness and rage it unleashed in me, common, I think, to many who grieve, though its expression is invariably individual and differently inflected in everyone – like all the many forms of agitation our minds and emotions are prey to, even those that find such precise description in the diagnostic manuals.

The journey invariably took me into the civil and political sphere where, outside the horrors of war, we expect ordinary reason to prevail. Not the reason that is an excluding hyper-rationality, better suited to the strict binaries and statistical accumulation of the cyber and economic sphere, which for humans is its own form of madness. But an aspiration of reason, the best of reason with its balanced judgements, its foresight, its forms and limits and, yes, its kindness. That may be an ideal but it's what allows society to function and provides us with the tempered state we need for life in all its variety to flourish. That world didn't seem to be where I remembered it: there was rage and madness everywhere. The politics of emotion ruled, effacing clarity, whipping up murderous hatreds.

I turned to home, family and friends for solace. The nursery was where I found it. Here, primal emotions are rife, and those endearingly crazy creatures we call children gambol. Here, too, were the germs of those states that had sadly run rampant in our polity. The passions and inner accommodations that shape character.

When I was a young woman, I used to think with what I can only call future nostalgia that old age would be a country I would like to travel in: a place on the other side of all those rapids of tormenting passion, on the far side of the abyss of anguishing uncertainties, the hillocks of squandered concentration on one's waist, thigh or eyebrow line. That ultimate certainty – death – was so close in the country of old age that a landscape of calm, wisdom, understanding, and the capacity for judgement would prevail. None of these were qualities often encountered on the home front.

My image of old age was something of a rash idealization, characteristic of youth itself. It was not uncoloured by W. B. Yeats's 'Sailing to Byzantium' in which 'The young/In one another's arms,' neglect all those 'Monuments of unageing intellect'.

Images of a serene and Olympian Simone de Beauvoir, who seemed utterly at peace with the lines on her face and her razor-sharp analytic intelligence, played into the picture. I hadn't read her *Coming of Age* back then, with its excoriating critique of the othering of the old, their invisibility in a world where 'society only cares about the individual, so long as they're profitable'. Nor did I know that the bodies that had once given us at least a modicum of intense pleasure lost their energy and their sensuous apparatus, only to catapult into painful fragility.

Maybe my wish to narrate the everyday madnesses I have here described is a way of reaching towards that earlier ideal I had of old age. Our best hopes of the country an increasing number of us now inhabit is – indignation aside – to allow some reconciliation with life, one's own too. And with death.

It was the love of a grandchild that put me on track. He led me to the passions of the nursery – those that underlie some of our everyday dislocations and excesses. This in turn led me back to John, who was himself preoccupied with such matters and shared that love. I wish he had been here to lift littlest Isaiah to his height and give him a view from that shoulder.

My rage against him has abated. And his ghost has grown calmer in turn. I can now read him with pleasure, look at photographs without going blind. He has become a friend again, rather than an alien enemy tearing at my entrails, forcing a deranged and punishing self-diminishment. I still sometimes want to be dead, but then I look at my admirable children and their lovely babes with all their passions. I think to myself, yes, these ordinary satisfactions of life – friendships, books, a pleasing vista or townscape, art – are quite extraordinary enough in themselves.

That is a great deal.

The small translucent bottle with its *Memory of Senses* no longer confronts me every day. I have moved it into a cabinet. When I examine its contents, they don't seem to be evaporating.

NOTES

p. v Svetlana Alexievich, *The Unwomanly Face of War*, Penguin, 2017, p. xvii.

p. v David Grossman, 'Israel is a Fortress, But Not Yet a Home', Memorial Day speech printed in *Haaretz* https://www. haaretz.com/israel-news/full-text-speech-by-david-grossman-at-alternative-memorial-day-event-1.6011820 on 20 May 2018.

GRIEVING

p. 3 John Berger, 'I think the dead are with us', *New Statesman* https://www.newstatesman.com/culture/2015/06/i-think-dead-are-us-john-berger-88 on 11 June 2015.

8

p. 33 Adam Zagajewski, 'Don't allow the lucid moment to dissolve', *Without End: New and Selected Poems* (trans. Renata Gorczynski), Farrar Strauss & Giroux, 2002.

10

p. 43 Sigmund Freud, 'Mourning and Melancholia', *The Standard Edition of the Complete Psychological Works of Sigmund Freud* vol. XIV (trans. and ed. James Strachey), Hogarth Press, 1957, p. 244.

p. 44 Freud, 'Thoughts on War and Death', SE14, p. 298.

p. 45 Adam Phillips, 'Against Self-Criticism', *London Review of Books*, 5 March 2015, pp. 13–16.

12

p. 51 Raymond Carver, 'Late Fragment', *A New Path to the Waterfall*, Atlantic Monthly Press, 1989.

13

p.56 John Bowlby, *Attachment and Loss* vol. 3, Hogarth Press, 1980, p. 104.

p. 57 Samuel Beckett, 'Krapp's Last Tape', *The Complete Dramatic Works*, Faber and Faber, 2006, p. 219.

p. 63 Phyllis Palgi and Henry Abramovitch, 'Death: A Cross-Cultural Perspective', *American Review of Anthropology* vol.13, October 1984, 385–417 http://www.annualreviews.org/doi/ abs/10.1146/annurev.an.13.100184.002125

p. 64 Donald Tuzin in 'The Breath of a Ghost', 1975, cited by Michele Stephen, *International Journal of Psychoanalysis* vol. 79, 1998, 1173–94 'Consuming the Dead: A Kleinian Perspective on Death Rituals Cross-Culturally'.

p. 64 Jack Goody, *Death, Property and the Ancestors: A Study of the Mortuary Customs of the Lodagaa of West Africa*, Tavistock Publications, 1962, p. 27.

LOSING

2

p. 88 Stated by James Williams on the podcast *Talking Politics*, 3 August 2017.

3

p. 94 Samuel Fishwick, 'City State of Mind', *Evening Standard*, 7 September 2017, pp. 20–21.

6

p. 100 Michel de Montaigne, *The Complete Essays* (trans. M. A. Screech), Allen Lane, 1991, p. 810.

p. 102 Elena Ferrante, *My Brilliant Friend* (trans. Ann Goldstein), Europa Editions, 2012, p. 83.

7

p. 105 Jean-Étienne Esquirol, *Mental Maladies: A Treatise on Insanity* (trans. E. K. Hunt, Lea and Blanchard), 1845, Google Books, p. 254.

10

p. 121 Adam Phillips, *Unforbidden Pleasures*, Hamish Hamilton, 2015, p. 56.

11

p. 124 Seneca, *De Ira* (Of Anger) I, 1–2, https://en. wikisource. org/wiki/Of_Anger/Book_I#I. Bohn's Classical Library Edition (trans. Aubrey Stewart), 1900, pp. 48–9.

p. 126 Adam Schatz, 'The Deep State', *London Review of Books*, 14 February 2017.

12

p. 128 I have narrated my mother's story more fully in *Losing the Dead* (Virago, 2013).

p. 134 Audre Lorde, 'Uses of Anger', *Your Silence Will Not Protect You*, Silver Press, 2018, pp 114–115.

16

p. 146 https://www.cbsnews.com/news/facebook-users-2-billion-biggest-countries/ on 8 April 2018.

p. 149 Alessandra Lemma, 'Psychoanalysis in times of technoculture: Some Reflections on the Body in virtual space', *International Journal of Psychoanalysis* vol. 96, 2015, 569–82.

LOVING

p. 181 Adam Phillips talking about *The Beast in the Nursery*, Faber & Faber, 1998.

5

p. 197 Marcel Proust, *In Search of Lost Time* (trans. Charles Scott-Moncrieff, D. J. Enright), Random House/Google Books, 1996; vol. 2 *Within a Budding Grove*, p. 283; vol. 3 *The Guermantes Way*, p. 397.

11

p. 221 Saint Augustine, *Confessions* (trans. R. Pine-Coffin), Penguin, 2003, pp. 27–8.

p. 222 Freud, SE 22, p. 122.

p. 226 Simone de Beauvoir, *Memoirs of a Dutiful Daughter* (trans. James Kirkup), Penguin, 1963, p. 12.

16

p. 246 John Forrester, 'Justice, Envy and Psychoanalysis', *Dispatches from the Freud Wars*, Harvard University Press, 1997, pp. 13–43.

ACKNOWLEDGEMENTS

I owe a huge debt of gratitude to my nearest family: my children, Josh and Katrina, their partners, Devorah Baum and Jamie Martin, and the grandchildren, Manny and now Isaiah. If they weren't there, I doubt this book would be. John's brothers, David and Andrew Forrester, and their wives, Helen and Jan, played their part, too. I thank them all, together with my close friends who provided those greatest of tonics, warmth and conversation. I can only mention a few: Adam Phillips, Gillian Slovo, Margie Orford (who was living upstairs at the time of John's death and whom I quote on p. 27), Marina Warner, Marino Craissatti, Maxine Molyneux, Michael Ignatieff, Susie Orbach, Suzette and Helder Macedo and Timberlake Wertenbaker.

The enthusiasm for this book from my agent, the great Tracy Bohan, has been invaluable. I thank her and my splendid editor at 4th Estate, Louise Haines, as well as Patrick Hargadon, Sarah Thickett and the team, and Hazel Orme.

CREDITS